KEYS TO BUYING A FORECLOSED HOME

Jack P. Friedman, Ph.D., C.P.A, M.A.I.
Dallas, Texas
and
Jack C. Harris, Ph.D.
Texas Real Estate Research Center
Texas A&M University
College Station, Texas

D1509819

BARRON'S

Jack P. Friedman is a real estate consultant in Dallas, Texas. Jack C. Harris is a research economist at the Real Estate Center of Texas A & M University. They are the authors of *Keys to Investing in Real Estate, Keys to Mortgage Financing and Refinancing,* and *Keys to Purchasing a Condo or Co-op,* and Mr. Friedman is the author of *Keys to Buying and Owning a Home* in Barron's Business Keys Series.

All inquiries should be addressed to:
Barron's Educational Series, Inc.
250 Wireless Boulevard
Hauppauge, New York 11788

Library of Congress Card No. 91-34291

International Standard Book No. 0-8120-4765-6

Library of Congress Cataloging-in-Publication Data

Harris, Jack C., 1945–
    Keys to buying a foreclosed home / Jack Harris and Jack Friedman.
    p.   cm. — (Barron's business keys)
    Includes index.
    ISBN 0-8120-4765-6
1. House buying.   2. Foreclosure.   3. Real estate investment.
I. Friedman, Jack P.   II. Title.   III. Series.
HD1390.5.H36   1992
332.63'24—dc20   91-34291
                                                                      CIP

PRINTED IN THE UNITED STATES OF AMERICA
2345   5500   98765432

CONTENTS

1

GETTING A HOME
FOR A BARGAIN

A home is probably the biggest investment you will make in your lifetime. If you can get a quality property that serves your purposes and save money in the process, you will reap important financial benefits.

In a home purchase a bargain is one bought for less than its market value. However, a property's market value is not easy to determine because information about the market is incomplete and transactions are relatively infrequent. The lack of market information provides opportunities to buy below market value, but creates pitfalls as well. Sellers generally know what they own, including its problems. A property may be a bargain because an uninformed seller is asking too little, or is anxious or desperate to sell. It may be a bargain because it was foreclosed and the lender/owner is under pressure to sell it quickly. In such cases, the more you know about market value, the better off you are.

It is possible to save a good deal of money in a home purchase in other ways as well. Unlike many things you buy, a home does not have an established, take-it-or-leave-it price. Even new homes are subject to negotiation between buyer and seller before a selling price is set. And there are several things that add up to that "price." A seller may agree to pay all or some of the items at closing that buyers normally pay, such as legal fees, appraisal fees, or discount points on a loan. There may be concessions in the contract that potentially add value to the home. Seller financing may be part of the deal, the terms of which can be tailored to add value.

Obviously, understanding the bargaining process and what makes a property more valuable helps when you are trying to negotiate a favorable price. Even more important is how anxious each party is to make a sale. In markets where there are many buyers and few homes available, the seller can hold out for top dollar. But in cases where buyers are hard to find and there are plenty of homes on the market, the buyer can bargain. When the seller is under pressure to move the property, the result is often termed a "distress sale." By finding and sizing up such sales, a home buyer can save a great deal of money.

This book serves as a guide to finding and taking advantage of distress sale situations. In most cases, distress sales follow when the property owner is in financial trouble and must sell the property. Many of these homes become foreclosed. Then the home generally goes into an inventory of repossessed homes, which eventually become available for sale. Holders of these homes may offer attractive deals to prospective buyers. The book explains the foreclosure process and how you can bid on homes at a foreclosure sale. Another section describes the types of holders of repossessed homes and how they go about liquidating these homes. Also included is a section on buying from these inventories. Many distressed properties are sold at auction, and a section details how a real estate auction works.

Distress properties may appeal to homebuyers who thought they could never afford a home (there are some of these special programs for buyers with below-average incomes) and to real estate investors looking for good income-producing property. However, some of these properties are in poor condition or are located in areas that limit their value. This book will help you to evaluate the opportunity and to follow through once you decide on a course of action.

2

THE HOME BUYING PROCESS

If you've never bought a home before, you may not be familiar with the steps required to make the purchase or even how to get started. Even if you already own a home, you may want to use this Key to review the general procedure.

Buying a home in a distress sale may be quite different from the typical purchase procedure. However, to appreciate how it differs, you should know the "normal" procedure. (Virtually every home purchase turns out to be an adventure and requires some extraordinary action by the buyer, seller, or both. Nevertheless, there is a sequence of steps that most buyers and sellers attempt to follow.)

At some point in time, you come to the conclusion that your present housing is no longer satisfactory. You begin a search of the housing market to see what is available. This can be done in many ways. You may visit a **broker** and inspect the homes currently listed for sale. Most brokers are members of **Multiple Listing Services**, which means they can show you most of the homes currently for sale in the area. In addition, you can check ads in the paper or watch for "for sale" signs in the neighborhoods that most appeal to you. Home builders may conduct **open houses** and employ a sales staff to show you their subdivisions.

After making a preliminary search, you begin to form an idea of which areas, or specific homes, you like as well as how much house you can afford to buy. This latter point is important, since it makes no sense to consider homes you can't afford. A broker can work with you to determine your borrowing limit or you can visit a mortgage lender for the same purpose. The amount of loan you can get is restricted by your income and any long-term debts you now have.

3

Once you have decided on a specific home, you begin the negotiation process with the owner. Generally, this begins when you make an offer to buy the home for a certain price. In the purchase of real estate, verbal offers are worthless. To make a serious offer, you submit it using a form called a **binder** or **sales contract** and include a cash deposit (called **"earnest money"**). If your offer is below the price listed by the seller, and it usually is, the seller is likely to not accept your offer but instead return a **counter-offer**. This may continue until both sides are satisfied or negotiations break down. The contract describes the rights of both buyer and seller, so make sure that everything you need is stated, including a **closing date** at which time the property will be transferred.

After the contract is signed, you need to arrange financing. Approval usually takes from four to eight weeks, depending on the type of financing sought. You should have included a **contingency** in the sales contract so that if the financing you need cannot be arranged, the sale is called off and you can reclaim the earnest money. With a signed sales contract, you can make a formal application for a loan with a lending institution or mortgage banker. Some sales are made without such financing when the buyer **assumes** the existing loan or the **seller** provides the **financing**. The lender must determine the value of the property by hiring an appraiser and **qualify** the buyer for the amount of loan applied for. If the buyer is approved, the lender forwards the required money to the closing where it is distributed to the seller with set amounts going to other parties who are to receive a fee.

At the closing, all money is exchanged and title to the property changes hands. Generally, a **title insurance company** is involved to assure that the buyer is receiving secure legal title to the property. There are various expenses, such as legal fees or real estate taxes, imposed upon either or both parties to the sale that are paid at closing. The closing marks the end of the home buying process.

3

HOW BUYING A FORECLOSED HOME IS DIFFERENT

In many cases, buying a foreclosed home is no different from buying any other home. Many holders of repossessed homes list them with real estate brokers and negotiate sales contracts just like other sellers. In fact, you may not even know that the home has been foreclosed until you find out who the seller is.

However, when holders sell their own inventory, the transaction may be quite different. Generally, these differences are in the way the property is advertised, the way purchase bids are handled, and the way sales contracts are negotiated. In addition, some holders sell properties in mass auctions. Buying at auction is discussed in Keys 31–35.

Holders of repossessed homes usually have large inventories of properties. In some cases, these homes are advertised in the classified section of local newspapers. Agencies like HUD take out large ads that describe several homes and provide a phone number for interested buyers to contact sales representatives.

There are special lists and computer printouts you can obtain that offer information on the entire inventory. You can call the agencies listed in the Appendix to get a copy; listings may be sorted by zip codes. There is usually a procedure to inspect the homes before submitting a bid even if you don't want to use a broker or sales agent. Often, inspections are conducted under the auspices of local agents employed to assist in the marketing effort.

Most government agencies have standard procedures that must be followed in making an offer on a home. Bids must be submitted on special forms available from the agency.

There may be an open bidding period during which submitted bids are collected and considered on a competitive basis. There can be a delay in response while bids are collected. There may be periods when certain types of buyers (such as people with limited income) are allowed to bid before other bids are considered. There may be restrictions on the price that can be submitted. For example, when the RTC first began selling homes, they required a bid of at least 95 percent of appraised value. You must contact the agency involved to get the proper forms and list of restrictions.

In some cases, you will need to have financing lined up before making a bid because there may not be provision for financing contingencies in the contract. A bidder is expected to complete the purchase when it is awarded. If you cannot do that, you may have to forfeit any deposit forwarded with the bid. A bid that is contingent on selling your current home will probably not be considered.

Cash buyers will receive priority. Some holders offer financing or other types of assistance as part of the transaction. In addition, you may be eligible for loan guarantees from the Federal Administration (FHA) or Veterans Administration (VA) if you qualify. Agencies may offer to pay some closing costs, but those costs are deducted from the amount you offer when the agency compares your bid to others.

Although you should be in a position to follow up quickly on your bid, you may have to be patient while you wait for the seller to respond. The person marketing the property or handling the bidding process may not have authority to accept offers without submitting them through an approval process. This is especially true when your bid is below the listed appraised value. Recognize that organizations often take longer to make decisions and act on them than individuals do. However, if the home is truly a good deal, your patience may be rewarded.

4

ADVANTAGES OF BUYING
A FORECLOSED HOME

The foremost attraction of distressed real estate is the prospect of finding a gem for a bargain price. The fact that a property has been foreclosed does not mean that something is wrong with it. In many cases, properties were bought at the top of a booming market, and the owners can no longer justify or afford excessive monthly payments on properties that have gone down in value. Often, buyers overextended themselves financially and finally had to relieve themselves of the burden. The same property with a more realistic price and debt load can be perfectly fine. But there are properties that are inappropriate for their surroundings, so poorly designed, or in such need of repair that they should be torn down. These, too, are subject to foreclosure. These are the ones you *don't* want.

You hope that you can buy a foreclosed property for a price below that prevailing in the current market. In cases where the holder has a large inventory and is aggressive in liquidating it, you may even get a real bargain price. However, an asking price that is below some amount previously paid for the home does not mean you are being offered a good deal. You have to compare the price with those of other similar properties on the market. There are cases where a holder is trying to get top dollar—perhaps at least the amount of the loan balance that was owed to them plus lost interest—making the home over-priced in today's market. As a bargain-hunting buyer, you must know a steal when you see it and move quickly—as you would to pick up a $20 bill that was dropped in the street. You must also know when the asking price is still too high. You become knowledgeable about values by constantly keeping up with the market, knowing what sold for how much and what is currently on the market at what price.

Another potential advantage of buying foreclosed inventory is that the holder is presumably anxious to deal. There should be no dickering over a move-in date, as may happen when the owner is still living in the home. Most foreclosed homes are vacant and represent a cash drain on the holder. A quick sale is valued and this may provide opportunities to deal.

Finally, some holders will provide inducements to make the property more attractive. Often some minor repair and remodeling will be done. More important are financial inducements. Some holders will pay part of the buyer's closing costs, such as discount points on a third-party loan. Some even offer to finance the property purchase, often at terms much better than those available in the market. You may have to pay a competitive price for the home to enjoy a bargain in the financing, but that bargain may be even more advantageous than an initial low price in the long run.

It is important to understand that these advantages are not guaranteed in all cases. Some holders insist on market value prices, present delays in transactions, and do not offer financing or any other inducement. You must be alert to what is available. (See Key 41.)

As an example, suppose you could choose between a 10 percent reduction in the price of the house you want to buy and a $1\frac{1}{2}$ percentage point reduction in the interest rate. The rate reduction is likely to be preferable for a long-term investment and a 30-year loan. Specifically the monthly payment on $90,000 at 10 percent is $789.81; on $100,000 at $8\frac{1}{2}$ percent it is $768.91.

5

DISADVANTAGES OF BUYING A FORECLOSED HOME

While the idea of getting a bargain home is appealing, there are some significant pitfalls to watch out for. As a consequence, the pursuit may not be for every home buyer or investor and would not serve the needs of many buyers. Above all the bargain hunter needs to know the market and the procedures for buying and be prepared to act when the opportunity arises. Not everyone has the time or flexibility to do this.

Timing is important. If a home is a true bargain, there will be competition among knowledgeable buyers. This means you could end up paying too much for the property. Many sales contracts for foreclosed homes do not include contingencies, so you must be prepared to complete the deal. In many cases, financing has to be arranged ahead of time. If the property requires substantial repair, financing may be hard to arrange, especially if it is to include funds for construction.

Condition is another concern. Most properties are offered on an "as is" basis. Many of these homes have been vacant for an extended period. Vacancy invites vandalism and usually means normal upkeep has been neglected. Some properties may even have been vandalized by the previous owners as a parting shot to vent their anger or frustration at being forced out through foreclosure. A particularly difficult situation arises when a large number of homes have been foreclosed in the same area. The neighborhood starts to look like a ghost town, with boarded-up windows and overgrown lawns. This not only hurts the neighborhood's reputation, but decreases the value of all property in the area.

Under normal conditions, foreclosures are rare, so the range of homes available is limited. You may not find a home that suits your needs. Where economic decline has made foreclosure more common, however, this is not such a problem. For example, in Texas there is a wide variety of homes available in most major metropolitan areas.

Depending on how the home is obtained, you may have a problem getting good title to the property. Most states give the borrower who loses his or her home at foreclosure the right to reclaim it upon paying the debt, interest, and costs. That right may extend well past the foreclosure sale. This is primarily a liability for buyers at foreclosure sales. However, there is some risk even when you buy from a lenders' inventory. Most holders will offer a special (limited) warranty deed at sale, and this does not provide the full protection provided by a general warranty deed. Hire a lawyer and get an opinion from him. Avoid a property with a title defect that could jeopardize your ownership rights. If possible, get a title insurance policy on the property.

Finally, much frustration can come from the sellers' seeming reluctance to respond to a bid. This is particularly a problem when you buy from government agencies. The process can become bogged down in red tape, rigid procedure, and over-management of the process of accepting offers. Often, you may need plenty of determination to buy such properties.

6

CAN YOU GET A BARGAIN HOME?

To get a bargain, you must be willing to spend the time and effort to become familiar with the market and investigate the property. Most people seeking foreclosed or distress sale property are hoping to get a good property at a steal. Some buyers indeed get exceptional values, taking advantage of situations that favor buyers and being in the right place at the right time. Others end up with properties that have more problems than expected, and eventually require so much additional investment that they, too, lose the homes to foreclosure. Then there are those who lose sight of why they are trying to buy a foreclosed home and pay too high a price in the competition to win the bidding.

The key to getting a bargain is knowing what you are getting and understanding what its value is in the market. Making "low ball" bids on any property available will probably not be successful. When it does work, you may be getting a property with so many problems that no other bidder was interested.

Most properties are offered "as is," but you have the opportunity to inspect the property before making a bid. You should always take advantage of this opportunity, even to the extent of hiring a professional inspector for properties you are serious about. Further, do your homework. You should consider the neighborhood, especially how it influences the value of the property and how appropriate it is for the use you intend. If the property is surrounded by other vacant buildings, understand that you are gambling on recovery of the area at some time in the near future. Any risk that you are forced to take should be reflected in the price you offer.

You should always have a reference value to compare against the price you are prepared to pay for the property.

The reference should be a comparable property in what you consider to be acceptable condition. You can estimate what it would take to make the property you are considering equal to the reference property. This amount should be deducted from the reference value when deciding on your "reservation price."

Your reservation price is the highest you should be willing to pay for the property. Consider the prices of other properties in the market, likely future opportunities to buy other properties, and how badly you want this one. Decide what price would be the most you would pay if you really had to. That amount is your reservation price. Write it on a piece of paper and do not allow yourself to pay more. You hope you can get the property for something less than your reservation price. If so, you may have gotten a true bargain. But never pay more than your reservation price even though it means not "winning" the bid.

You may even want to have an appraisal done on the property (see Key 44). This will tell you what comparable properties have sold for recently. The cost of the appraisal ($200–$300) can be worth it if it keeps you from making a costly error and paying too much for the property. Another approach is to include in the contract that the house must appraise for at least the amount you agree to pay. If it appraises for less than the contract, you can negotiate a lower price or walk away from the deal.

Holders of foreclosed homes are receiving little or no benefit from keeping the property in inventory. Therefore, they should be anxious to sell. However, they do want to get as high a price as possible. They may be willing to hold the property rather than sell it for less than they consider obtainable in the market. Sometimes you can get a bargain if you quickly satisfy what the holder needs. That may mean having the cash or prearranged financing to swing the deal. It may mean being able to complete the transaction without delay.

7

BUYING FOR INVESTMENT VERSUS HOMEOWNERSHIP

How you approach foreclosed real estate depends on whether you are looking for a property to live in or to rent out. To some extent, your situation will have a lot to do with whether you should consider distressed property at all.

When you buy a property to be your home, your primary concern is whether the property can provide the type of home environment you want. First, you want to locate in an area that is relatively convenient to your place of work and other areas you visit frequently. You want a neighborhood that is reasonably secure and a good place to raise a family or to do whatever your personal life style entails. In general, an area where homeowners keep their properties in good order and where industrial, commercial, and heavy traffic is at a minimum helps protect the value of your investment. Finally, the home itself should be attractive and provide enough space for your needs.

For investment property, your focus is different. You want a property that can be rented for enough to cover expenses and provide some return. Only under special circumstances should you rely on appreciation in value to provide a return on your investment. The property should provide "cash flow"—that is, rental income must exceed out-of-pocket costs. Look for factors that might make it hard for you to keep the property rented. These include undesirable features that drive away tenants or cause a lot of turnover. For example, a high crime area would repel good tenants and leave you with those to whom you might not want to rent. If the neighborhood is not well kept, the value of your property may decline unless the opportunity arises to convert to another use.

If you are buying a house that will be your home, you may be coming to the transaction with extra baggage. You may currently be obligated on a lease or own a home that must be sold before you can buy the new home. If this is the case, you may not be in a good position to bid for foreclosed property. Many sellers will not entertain offers contingent on the sale of other property. If you require approved financing, you face a handicap in competing with other buyers. Finally, many properties are offered "as is," and you may not be able to get a guarantee of good working order.

As an investor, on the other hand, you are probably in a better position to deal. However, you must still do your homework before negotiation and be ready to make a solid offer when an opportunity arises. You may even be able to identify several acceptable properties. Then you can go for the one that turns out to represent the best value. In that way, you will be less likely to overpay because you became wedded to one property.

A good approach to use as an investor is to determine whether the property will provide a cash flow. You can figure how much the monthly payments will be, and see whether rent will cover them. For example, suppose you will have the following monthly payments:

Principal and Interest	$500.
Taxes	75.
Insurance	50.
Repairs, painting, maintenance	75.
Monthly requirements	$700.

If the property is not expected to rent for more than $700, you better pass it up because you will experience negative cash flow. Buy it only if it is likely to appreciate in value or provide other benefits in the future.

8

WHY HOMES ARE FORECLOSED

Lenders are willing to make home mortgage loans for fairly large amounts and at fairly low rates of interest because a valuable piece of property makes good collateral. When you get a loan to buy a home, you sign two important documents. The first—the note—describes your obligation to repay the loan each month. The second—the mortgage contract—gives the lender certain legal rights to the home in case you fail to fulfill your obligation to repay the loan. Without the home as collateral securing the loan, no lender would consider giving you such a large loan.

Of course, not everyone who signs a mortgage contract is able to live up to the financial obligation. Loss of a job, a major financial loss, or an unexpected burden could render a borrower insolvent and unable to continue making payments. Most mortgage contracts allow a grace period of ten to fifteen days after a payment is due before a penalty is added to the payment, and the loan is soon considered delinquent. When payments are generally three or more months behind, the loan is considered in default and the borrower is notified of the consequences of not keeping up with the payments. Local lenders sometimes work with borrowers who are having difficulty because of job loss or some other hardship, especially when it is obviously temporary. However, many loans are merely serviced by local lenders, having been bought by a national institutional investor. These investors apply general policies to all loans and do not allow the local servicer to deviate from policy. After default, a lender's next step is to accelerate the loan (declare the full amount to be due immediately, not just the missed payments) and start foreclosure proceedings.

A loan can be in default and subject to foreclosure for any

breach of the mortgage contract. For example, failing to insure a property adequately is a default of the mortgage contract. However, almost all foreclosures are the result of not making loan payments on time.

Although financial difficulty usually is at the root of delinquent payments, a homeowner who is unable to make payments could often sell the house and pay off the loan. However, if market conditions are not right, the borrower may not be able to sell the home for enough to cover the mortgage balance and the expenses of a sale. That is why home foreclosures are so frequent when local economies go into recession. Not only are people thrown out of work and incomes decreased, but market values of homes fall. Under these conditions, homeowners have been known to simply mail their house keys to the lender in lieu of the monthly payment. Still, they may be liable for the difference between their debt and the eventual sales price at foreclosure, called a "deficiency judgment."

When a lender accelerates the loan, the borrower has a certain amount of time to respond to this mandate. Foreclosure is the process by which the lender turns to the collateral property to satisfy the outstanding debt. The procedures used and the rights available to the borrower are established by state law and may differ markedly from state to state. The next several Keys describe various steps in the process in general terms. For your particular state, you will need to consult an attorney familiar with local law.

Author's note: Keys 9 through 13 provide information about foreclosures that may be helpful in understanding the process, but is not essential to the potential home buyer. The home buyer needs assurance from a qualified attorney or title company as to the quality of title being received, and any risks assumed. The home buyer must not assume those risks nor rely on information provided here as sufficient to avoid legal difficulties with acquisitions.

9

JUDICIAL FORECLOSURE

Rights of mortgage lenders and borrowers have evolved over time. The basic premise is to allow the lender to protect its investment in the event that the borrower fails to live up to the mortgage agreement. At the same time, the law aims to protect the borrower from a lender who wants to wrest away the mortgaged property wrongfully. We all have in mind a picture of the unscrupulous lender pouncing on a helpless borrower by claiming valuable property at the first sign of economic trouble. However, most lenders are more comfortable making loans than managing property and would prefer their borrowers to simply keep their loans current. When it becomes evident that the borrower is unable or unwilling to honor the obligation, all any lender wants to do is salvage whatever amount is possible from the collateral.

Foreclosure law is formed and enforced at the state level. For that reason, specific approaches to the problem of allocating rights between lender and borrower vary in each state. However, states fall into one of two categories of legal philosophy. The majority of the states subscribe to the idea that a mortgage establishes a special interest in the property known as a lien. In the event of a default on the mortgage obligation, the lender may exercise a claim on the property that is satisfied in court proceedings. Other states provide the lender with rights similar to those of an owner of the property. In these states, the law establishes procedures for the sale of the property in the case of default. In general, lenders in these states are in a stronger position to protect their interests than those in states following the lien philosophy. As a practical matter, the procedures of foreclosure and sale of the property have a similar effect in all states.

At one time, a borrower who was delinquent on a loan

17

payment would have to forfeit all rights to the property, which became the property of the lender. This "strict fore-closure" has been phased out in many states in favor of law that provides the borrower a specified "equity of redemption." This means that the borrower has the right to redeem the property by satisfying the debt. When a lender foreclos-es a loan, it is this equity of redemption that is being fore-closed, or eliminated. All states provide borrowers with some period of time during which the borrower can avoid losing the property by paying off the loan, but the length of this period varies.

A lender who wants to foreclose petitions the court to cut off this period. In most cases, the borrower is allowed to occupy the property and may even sell it during this period. In some states, the mortgage contract provides that the lender can put the property up for sale in the event of a default; in others, the sale must be conducted under the sanction of the court. This latter procedure is referred to as "judicial foreclo-sure." It is a relatively time consuming and expensive pro-cess that virtually guarantees that the lender will be unable to fully satisfy the debt through sale proceeds. However, the purchaser of the property at the foreclosure sale, usually the lender, is assured of receiving a property free and clear of all encumbrances.

Lenders typically acquire the property at foreclosure although they would prefer a sale. Lenders can simply pre-sent their lien to acquire the property. Another party could bid more than the unpaid debt, taking the property away from the lender. However, the lender cannot profit from the foreclosure sale. Any excess over the sum of the unpaid debt plus back interest and foreclosure costs goes to the former owner.

10

NON-JUDICIAL FORECLOSURE

In many states, the customary mortgage contract is worded to allow the lender to sell the property in the case of foreclosure without going through an extended court process. Such "power of sale" mortgages make it easier for the lender to recover the debt. Though the rights of the owner are not fully protected by the courts, these "non-judicial" foreclosures are commonly used where state law allows.

In some states (California, Colorado, Mississippi, Missouri, Tennessee, Texas, Oregon, Virginia, West Virginia, and the District of Columbia), the predominant type of mortgage used is the deed of trust. This mortgage provides for a trustee who is granted the power to sell the property in the event of default and foreclosure. The trustee must conduct the sale under strict guidelines established in the law of the state. However, the process is straightforward and is more predictable than the alternative of a court monitored sale. (The disadvantage of not involving the courts is that it may leave the action open to later challenge and scrutiny by the courts. This is rarely the case, however, when the rules are clear and are followed strictly.)

The trustee must provide public notice of the sale. In most jurisdictions there is a certain time and place for the sale, most often the county courthouse on a designated day each month. If you are interested in participating, check periodically with the county clerk for notices of impending sales. Courthouses will have a bulletin board where notice of each property to be foreclosed is posted for several weeks before the sale. However, the notice may provide only a legal description that is adequate to locate the property on a survey map, and not describe its size, features, or condition. You have no right to visit private property just because it has been

19

posted for foreclosure. However, the owners may invite you to visit if your intention is to purchase from them.

Foreclosure destroys all mortgage liens established after the time of the mortgage being foreclosed. Therefore, the buyer receives the property free and clear of the subject mortgage, as well as any mortgages that may have been added later. However, any claims established before the first mortgage was created are still in effect. It is important to have the title searched and to gain the protection provided by title insurance, especially when purchasing foreclosed property.

States where non-judicial foreclosure sales are typically used include: Alabama, Alaska, Georgia, Idaho, Maryland, Massachusetts, Minnesota, New Hampshire, New York, Rhode Island, South Dakota, and Wyoming. Also included are those states where the deed of trust is the predominant mortgage instrument (listed earlier).

11

DEED IN LIEU OF FORECLOSURE

All defaults need not result in foreclosure sales. In some cases, a borrower faced with foreclosure may be able to sell the property prior to losing it. The new owner may be able to assume the old mortgage and bring it up to date. More often, the buyer will arrange new financing and retire the old loan. A distressed owner may have an incentive to sell even though the price is below the mortgage balance owed, since a foreclosure may destroy his or her ability to get another mortgage loan. In many cases, however, the owner cannot afford or is unwilling to sell a home for less than what is owed.

Some borrowers are under the impression that they can merely turn ownership over to the lender and thereby satisfy the debt. During economically depressed periods, it is not uncommon for homeowners to mail in the keys to their homes instead of making up the mortgage payments. However, a lender does not have to accept such a transfer in payment for the debt. There is a good chance that in the ensuing foreclosure sale, the property will not sell for enough to cover the debt plus expenses. In that case, the borrower may still be liable for a deficiency judgment for the difference.

On the other hand, sometimes lenders do accept the transfer. Title to the property goes to the lender in a transaction termed "deed in lieu of foreclosure." When the lender accepts such a deed, the right to a deficiency judgment is waived. In these cases, the lender has determined that possessing the property without delay is preferable to the cost and risk of pursuing both a foreclosure proceeding and a deficiency judgment suit. Often, the borrower is "judgment proof," meaning that he or she has little wealth available to satisfy a judgment, even if successful in court.

What this means to the buyer seeking foreclosed property is that some homes may become part of a lender's inventory without going through a foreclosure sale. While you may not have the opportunity to bid at a foreclosure sale on these properties, you may be able to buy from the lender's inventory (see Keys 25–30). One thing you should recognize about such properties is that the deed in lieu of foreclosure process may not resolve all claims against the property. Therefore, when buying from lender's inventory, it is important to receive a warranty deed to protect against future claims against the property.

12

FORECLOSURE SALES

The end result of a foreclosure proceeding is a sale of the property. Money from the sale goes to satisfy the outstanding debt plus accrued interest and expenses. If there is any money remaining, it is used to pay any junior lien holders on the property and, finally, the borrower. If, as often happens, the proceeds are not enough to cover the debt, a deficiency judgment may be brought against the borrower.

The foreclosure sale is conducted as an open auction where anyone interested in the property may enter a bid. Procedures for conducting a sale are set by the courts or within state law and vary from state to state. However, some features are universal. Adequate notice of the time and place of the sale, as well as a description of the property, must be given to both the borrower and the public. This may include an official notice at the county courthouse and some type of advertisement in the local legal newspaper. This is to insure that the public is notified of the sale and any interested party may bid. Procedures used for entering bids and accepting a winner are written in the law as well.

When a judicial foreclosure is used, the sale is conducted under the instructions and supervision of the courts. In some states, a minimum acceptable price will be set by the court. In all cases, the court must accept the results of the sale before it is finalized. This requirement is to protect the borrower from a large deficiency judgment resulting from too low a sales price.

Non-judicial foreclosure sales are conducted by the trustee or designated person in the mortgage contract. Procedures are described in the contract and are consistent with state law. There is some potential that non-judicial sales will be set aside because of a challenge from the borrower.

However, most borrowers who feel aggrieved by the sales proceedings will sue for damages rather than to set aside the sale. Therefore, as a practical matter, non-judicial sales are as safe for the successful bidder as are judicial sales.

In almost all foreclosure sales, the lender is the successful bidder on the property. A lender may bid a specific dollar amount or simply present the debt owed as the amount bid. Outside bidders are encouraged to bid so that the sale is more fair and less likely to be challenged. The winning bidder receives the property in the same legal condition the property was in prior to the making of the mortgage. The foreclosed mortgage and any junior mortgages made afterwards are eliminated. However, the title may still be clouded by any right of redemption provided to the borrower by state law. This can be a serious drawback to bidders in states that provide a lengthy right of redemption.

An individual investor may feel intimidated bidding against institutions at a foreclosure sale. Most lenders, however, will be pleased to see the property go to an outside party, alleviating them of the trouble of receiving the property and reselling it. Their primary objective will be to assure that the winning bid is not too low that they do not receive what is owed on the mortgage. If you feel confident that the property can be obtained at a good price, bid. You may find it more advantageous, however, to buy from the lender after the sale is consummated.

13

THE QUALITY OF TITLE RECEIVED AT A FORECLOSURE SALE

One reason for hesitation about buying at a foreclosure sale is concern over title to the property. Depending on how the sale is conducted and on state law, the buyer may have a perfectly good deed or may face the possibility of losing the property in a legal dispute. You should check carefully with an attorney and title company, and not buy if there is any doubt of good title.

First of all, recall that foreclosure by the mortgage holder effectively cuts off the rights of the borrower to the property and eliminates the mortgage lien. It also eliminates any subordinate mortgages or liens created after the subject mortgage (except for tax liens held by local government and vendors liens that may be held by anyone who worked on the property without being paid in full). If you purchase the property at the foreclosure sale, you obtain the same rights enjoyed by the borrower before the loan was made.

There are several potential limitations to these rights, however. First, you will probably receive a special warranty deed at the sale. This type of deed guarantees that any claims to the property that were created while the seller owned it have been cleared. However, it makes no promises about claims arising before the property was foreclosed. Be wary of a quit claim deed, as it provides no guarantee. In such a deed the grantor gives up whatever rights he or she has, but may not actually have any ownership rights at all.

Second, if the property was not foreclosed under the supervision of the courts, there is a chance that the sale will be challenged and thrown out. This could result from failure to follow the procedures provided in the law or because the winning bid is considered not to be a fair price for the property. As mentioned in the previous Key, borrowers who challenge a sale generally seek damages rather than to nullify the sale, so the chances of losing the property are small. In any case, beware of a situation where the winning bid appears ridiculously low.

From the time a mortgage is declared in default to the time it is foreclosed, the borrower has an equitable right of redemption. That means the borrower could prevent the foreclosure sale by paying back the loan plus accrued interest. Once the lender accelerates the loan, the option of merely bringing the payments up to date is lost. However, in many states, the borrower retains the right to redeem the property even after foreclosure and sale of the property. This is called the statutory right of redemption and can vary by state from zero to many months.

The possibility that the borrower could reclaim the property can be a nuisance to anyone who buys at the sale. While the chances of a previous owner actually redeeming the property are remote, you may have concerns about renovation, repair, and remodeling of the structure. Before bidding at a foreclosure sale, you should know what kind of right of redemption is provided borrowers in your state. If it is a lengthy period of time, you may want to avoid foreclosure sales and focus your efforts on properties that have been acquired by lenders, their "Real Estate Owned" (REO) inventory.

14

AFTER THE
FORECLOSURE SALE

In most states, the lender is allowed to bid on the property at the foreclosure sale. In fact, the lender is often the only serious bidder and ends up with the property. The lender presents the mortgage debt as a bid on the property and obtains it with no additional cash expense. Other bidders must come up with cash or arrange financing for the price of the property. In addition, questions about the quality of the title may discourage outside bidders. In states that provide a lengthy right of redemption, the possibility of the property reverting to a previous owner is an additional deterrent.

The courts recognize the possibility that a foreclosure sale may not yield a fair price and often attempt to set a minimum price for the property. A price that is too low will make the borrower liable for an unfairly large deficiency judgment. For example, in Texas a lender must be prepared to show that the highest bid is at least 70 percent of the property's market value. This raises the possibility that the sale will be inconclusive if no one is willing to bid the minimum. In most cases, the lender wishes to avoid an inconclusive sale (as well as ward off challenge suits by the borrower) and may offer the minimum to acquire the property.

In today's complex residential financial market, the present lender is not always the entity that originally made the loan. Many home loans are originated (first made) by mortgage banking companies. Mortgage bankers package the loans they originate and sell them on what is called the "secondary" mortgage market. This market has grown rapidly in recent years especially by accommodating savings and loan associations, which, until recently, customarily kept the loans they originated. The secondary mortgage market (not to be confused with second mortgages) handles trading for the majority of first mortgages, as these are often traded within a few days after origination. Although the mortgage banker or savings and loan association continues to service the loan (collect payments and maintain the escrow account) the loan is actually owned by someone else. This may be a private investor that buys loans. In most cases, the loan is one in a large pool of loans held by a specialized secondary market entity. The largest of these entities were created by the federal government, but are privately owned. The Federal National Mortgage Association, or Fannie Mae, holds most of its loans in a large portfolio. The Federal Home Loan Mortgage Corporation, or Freddie Mac, sells portions of its portfolio to investors. Each of these organizations, but especially Fannie Mae, may be the initiator and winning bidder at a foreclosure sale on loans it holds.

You may have heard of Ginnie Mae, nickname for the Government National Mortgage Association (GNMA), though its role in foreclosures is minimal. Ginnie Mae is a government agency that subsidizes loans made to qualified low income homeowners.

Loans that are insured or guaranteed involve additional entities when they are foreclosed. When a loan is guaranteed by the Federal Housing Administration (FHA) or a private mortgage insurance company, the lender has a claim against the insurer when the borrower defaults. The insurer may pay off the amount of the claim and leave the lender to foreclose. However, often the insurer finds it better to acquire the property and try to recoup losses through resale. The Veterans' Administration (VA), which guarantees loans for qualified veterans, may either pay off the amount of the guarantee or acquire the property. When the property is foreclosed they may offer "no-bid," meaning that they pay their guarantee to the mortgage lender, usually serviced by a mortgage banker. That can load up a mortgage banker with unwanted property that may be sold as a forced sale.

Savings and loan (S&L) associations and commercial banks (CB) are covered by insurance that protects depositors in the event of insolvency by the institution. In many cases, the Federal Deposit Insurance Corporation (FDIC), which is the government agency providing the insurance, acquires the assets of the failing bank, including properties previously repossessed by the institution and non-performing loans on properties that will soon be foreclosed. Because of extensive failures during the latter part of the 1980s, a new government organization, the Resolution Trust Corporation (RTC), was created to liquidate these properties. In some states, the holdings of this organization are large and varied.

When lenders, companies, and government organizations acquire properties, they place them in special inventories. For lending institutions, this inventory is called "real estate owned" (REO) or "other real estate owned" (OREO). These terms refer to real estate the bank owns other than the property it needs to conduct its banking business.

These organizations attempt to manage the properties to produce whatever income possible, but their intent is to sell them off as expeditiously as possible. They may advertise and take bids, list with professional brokers, or hold auctions. These inventories are the richest source of potential bargain properties available. However, each organization has its own operating procedures and the prospective buyer must be familiar with them. The procedures of the major holders of REO are described in the next Key.

15

LENDING INSTITUTIONS

Savings and loan associations, commercial banks and even some credit unions make home mortgage loans. Today, many of these loans are sold into the secondary market. However, a sizable proportion are held in portfolio by the lending institution. When defaults occur on these loans, the institution ends up obtaining the property in most instances. The properties are placed in an REO inventory to be managed and resold to the public.

The methods used to sell REO properties may vary with each institution. In fact, one institution may use a variety of methods over time, depending on the size of its inventory and what seems to be working at the time.

If the inventory is relatively small, as it is under normal conditions, the institution will probably grant exclusive listings with local real estate brokers. An exclusive listing gives one broker the right to sell the property for a commission to the exclusion of all other brokers. This provides the security necessary to allow the broker to advertise the listing. Other brokers work with the listing broker, when the listing broker belongs to a multiple listing service.

When the inventory is unusually large, it may be worthwhile for the institution to establish an in-house management and sales staff. If a large number of properties are of the same type or are located in the same area, the institution may hold an auction.

Therefore, there are a number of ways to bid upon REO property. You may go directly to lending institutions in your area and inquire about currently available homes. You may ask a local broker about homes being sold by lending institutions. (Recognize that a broker's responsibility is to the seller. Ethically, the broker should not disclose details about the seller's need to sell the property. However, the identity of the seller can be disclosed. In fact, brokers will often tell prospective buyers that the owner is an institution that would like to dispose of the property quickly.) Lastly, you may participate in auctions conducted by lending institutions.

In most cases, you will find that institutions act much like any other property sellers. There are government-mandated regulations on how they sell properties that can lead to advantages and disadvantages for the buyer.

Advantages. The institution will be relatively anxious to sell the home. The home is probably vacant and not producing any income for the lender. In addition, the lender may have remodeled and repaired the building to make it more presentable. The lender may be willing to make special financing available on the purchase. These factors work in favor of the buyer.

Disadvantages. The biggest disadvantage is that the lender may be slow to respond to offers from potential buyers. There may be some type of administrative committee that must approve sales, especially when the bid is below appraised value. This can be frustrating for the bidder. There also may be a minimum price the lender is determined to get. It may be that the lender is trying to avoid declaring a loss on the loan. A reservation price that is too high may stall the negotiations, although the lender may be able to counter the higher price with favorable financing terms.

The drawbacks do not rule out this avenue to bargain homes. Indeed, lending institution REO inventories are normally one of the best sources of repossessed homes. You will need to understand the ways in which the negotiation can stall and be prepared to offer ways around the problem.

16

BUYING FROM THE FEDERAL HOUSING ADMINISTRATION

The Federal Housing Administration (FHA) provides insurance against default on home mortgage loans. When covered by this insurance, a lender may provide a loan that supplies more than the standard 80 percent of the purchase price of a home. When defaults do occur, FHA often ends up with the home following the foreclosure sale. Because FHA provides insurance on low-downpayment loans, defaults are more common than on conventional loans. This means HUD usually has one of the larger inventories of repossessed homes.

Sometimes known as "HUD homes," these properties are offered for sale to the public (FHA is a division of the Department of Housing and Urban Development, or HUD). You may obtain a list of available homes from your local HUD field office (see Appendix) or go through a real estate broker. The agency does not in general use exclusive listings with brokers but will accept bids through brokers who are on an approved list.

Occasionally, HUD will place advertisements in the classified section of local newspapers. (Don't be confused with the reference to HUD rather than FHA. While FHA handles the insurance program, HUD is the parent agency that markets and sells the properties.)

Most homes will be offered with an asking price stated. Since there is a limit on the amount of loan that can be covered by FHA insurance, the homes held by HUD will be somewhat modest relative to the market. Homes may include condominiums and even some multi-family buildings. The agency generally does not repair or remodel the properties, except in cases of dangerous situations. If a home is in good enough condition to satisfy FHA standards, a purchase loan on the property may be eligible for insurance coverage. The FHA does not make loans directly and, therefore, does not finance the properties it sells.

Once you have inspected the property and decided on an offering price, you may submit a sealed bid to HUD. General procedure calls for holding all bids for the first 10 days after a property is offered. When the bids are opened, the highest net offer is accepted. In the case of a tie, the buyer who will occupy the home is given preference. Bids must be accompanied by an earnest money deposit of $500–2,000 depending on the asking price. This deposit is returned if the bid is rejected. Generally, there are no contingencies allowed for financing or other purposes.

A bid should state the offering price and any special costs to be incurred by HUD. The agency will pay some of the buyer's closing costs and any brokerage commission on the sale. However, these costs are deducted from the bid price for the purpose of determining the highest net to HUD bid. For example, someone offering $30,000 with no cost to HUD would beat out a bid of $31,000 calling for HUD to pay a commission of $1,500.

The bidding process is straightforward. On the other hand, properties must be examined carefully, for they may be in poor condition. Don't expect a luxury home in the inventory, but you may find some good income property. Finally, HUD provides no financing but the FHA may provide insurance on a loan you arrange with a lending institution or mortgage banker.

17

BUYING FROM THE VETERANS ADMINISTRATION

The Veterans Administration (VA) guarantees home loans for eligible military veterans. When a veteran defaults on the loan, the VA often buys the home in lieu of paying out the amount of the guarantee. When mortgage foreclosures have been frequent in an area, the VA is a good source of foreclosed homes. Addresses of VA Regional Offices are provided in the Appendix.

The VA markets homes in a similar fashion to HUD (see Key 16). Bids are accepted from the public (they may be entered through a real estate broker or directly), properties are offered in "as is" condition, bids must be submitted without contingencies, and a five- to ten-day waiting period is used to collect bids. However, there are some important differences.

The VA does not give brokers exclusive contracts to list properties, but it does designate a managing broker to coordinate sales of properties in an area. You may go directly to this broker or work through a broker of your choice. Unlike the FHA, the VA does not deduct the broker's commission from the bid price. However, you must offer the list price for a property unless it is designated for a negotiated price.

Another important distinction is that the VA will finance the homes it sells. These loans are fixed-rate loans at the current VA ceiling interest rate. Downpayment requirements are low, in many cases as low as 5 percent of the price. Furthermore, you do not have to be an eligible veteran to qualify for this financing.

If you have cash or have arranged financing elsewhere, the VA offers discounts for cash bids. Recently, these discounts were as much as 10 percent of the list price. In addition, the

VA will pay some of the closing costs for cash bids (this usually consists of paying all or some of the discount points on a loan from a third party). Finally, cash offers are approved more quickly than those calling for seller financing.

Homes held by the VA may be comparable in quality and size to those owned by the FHA. The primary advantage of buying from the VA is the possibility of getting favorable financing with a low downpayment. The tradeoff is that you may have to bid list price for the home.

Brokers will have a special form on which to submit an offer for a VA-home. Preferential treatment is accorded those who will occupy the residence as a home (but investors may also bid) and those who make larger down payments may receive a lower interest rate. Discovering how much the previous owner owed upon default is irrelevant. Once the VA forecloses, a new ball game begins, based on the appraised value of the home the VA gets, as provided by a real estate appraiser.

18

BUYING FROM THE FARMERS HOME ADMINISTRATION

The Farmers Home Administration (FmHA) makes loans and insures loans to farmers and residents of rural areas (including towns of up to 20,000 population) for the purchase of farms, land, and homes. The stated purpose of the home loan programs is to supplement private mortgage credit in areas that may not be adequately served otherwise. Because the loans covered by FmHA are low downpayment loans to borrowers of limited means, it is not unusual for defaults and foreclosures to occur. Consequently, if you are looking for property in the countryside or in a small town, FmHA may be a good place to check. A list of FmHA state offices is offered in the Appendix to this book.

Anyone may bid on property held by the FmHA, but the agency offers distinct advantages to those who qualify for their loan assistance program (see Key 36). In general, to be eligible, you must be a U.S. citizen, have low to moderate income (check with the local office for specific criteria), be able to qualify under FmHA loan requirem   , and be unable to obtain a loan elsewhere.

The FmHA prefers to enter into exclusive listing contracts with local brokers, so you should seek out a broker to find out what is available. The local office should be able to direct you to the appropriate broker. The agency accepts bids for 5 days on a new listing before opening them. You must bid at least the asking price for the property. However, the agency has a policy of reducing the price every 75 days until the property is sold.

The main advantages for those who qualify for the program are in the condition of the property and in financing.

36

The agency will fix up homes to make them available for immediate occupancy by those who meet eligibility requirements of the FmHA. For others, all properties are offered as is.

Financing for those eligible for the program is very favorable. No downpayment is required and loan terms may extend as long as 38 years. Borrowers may qualify for below-market interest rates and payment moratoriums as well. Financing is also available for non-eligibles on slightly less favorable terms. Such buyers must pay a minimum downpayment equal to 2 percent of the purchase price. The longest term allowed is 30 years for owner-occupants and 10 years for investors (a 20-year amortization term may be used with a balloon payment after the 10-year term). All bids must be accompanied by a $50 earnest money deposit, which is refundable if the bid is rejected by FmHA.

In evaluating bids, the agency gives priority to program eligibles. In fact, only eligible buyers may bid for the first 45 days after either a new listing or when a price reduction has been made. The object is to try to keep the properties in the FMHA program. However, when no acceptable bidders are found, the agency will liquidate the property in whatever way is possible.

19

BUYING FROM
MORTGAGE INSURANCE
COMPANIES

In general, before a lender will make a low-downpayment loan, the loan must either be guaranteed by the VA or FmHA or be covered by private mortgage (default) insurance. Before the FHA began offering such insurance, there were private companies that served this role. During the housing boom following World War II, private mortgage insurers were relatively inactive compared to the FHA. In recent years, the companies have regained presence in the market, mainly because of the limits placed on the size of loan FHA can insure.

Private mortgage insurance works much like FHA insurance. The main difference is that private insurance covers losses up to only 20 percent of the loan, whereas the FHA generally stands behind the entire loan amount. When a borrower on a loan covered by private insurance defaults, the lender forecloses and takes title at the foreclosure sale. The lender then files a claim with the insurance company for a portion of total losses incurred. The insurance company has the choice of taking title to the property by paying the entire loan or reimbursing the lender by the amount of the claim and letting the lender keep the property.

Because of their limited exposure to loss, private insurers do not take title to as many properties as does the FHA or VA. Nevertheless, these companies may be worth investigating, particularly if there is a headquarters in your area. The oldest, and largest, is the Mortgage Guaranty Insurance Corporation (MGIC). These insurance companies may use a variety of marketing methods and have no rigid procedures for entertaining bids. You may contact the company directly for information, particularly if there have been a large number of foreclosures in the area lately, or look for ads in the paper. Many properties are higher in quality and price than those held by the FHA and VA.

Private mortgage insurers are motivated sellers who know that they lose money by holding vacant property. They have less administrative red tape than government agencies and fewer properties to monitor. Consequently, they may be much easier to deal with and may have property that appeals to your tastes. However, their inventory will be much smaller than that of government agencies.

There is a popular misconception that mortgage insurance serves to protect the life of the borrower. The kind of mortgage insurance referred to here is default insurance, which has nothing to do with life insurance. As the term implies, default insurance is used to insure the lender in the event of a default. The borrower pays the cost, generally when the down payment is under 20 percent. Mortgage default insurance costs vary with the down payment. For a typical 10 percent down payment, the cost is 2 percent of the full amount borrowed at closing, and an annual charge of $1/4$ of 1 percent of the loan, in addition to all interest and principal payments.

Life insurance to the extent of the loan amount is often available to home owners, and may also be called mortgage insurance, though it is more precisely called mortgage life insurance. Its purpose is to pay off the loan if the bread-winner dies, so the surviving family household members can live debt-free. Often, term insurance is available at a lower cost and will provide the same protection. Nevertheless, the type of mortgage insurance company referred to in this Key offers mortgage default insurance, not life insurance.

20

BUYING FROM THE FEDERAL DEPOSIT INSURANCE CORPORATION

The Federal Deposit Insurance Corporation (FDIC) is a government agency created to insure deposit accounts at commercial banks. You probably have seen signs at your local bank advertising this coverage. When a bank fails, the FDIC moves in and either arranges a merger with a healthy bank or closes down the institution and takes over the bank. In either case, the FDIC obtains the assets of the failed institution (in merger cases, the FDIC may take assets the merging bank does not want). These assets include any REO held by the bank.

At one time, the Federal Savings and Loan Insurance Corporation (FSLIC) was the insurer for savings and loan associations. When FSLIC became insolvent in the late 1980s, its responsibilities were transferred to the FDIC. A new agency, the Resolution Trust Corporation (RTC), was created in 1989 to manage the process of shutting down failed savings and loans and liquidating seized assets. However, the FDIC retained control of all assets seized before 1989, as well as any assets obtained from failed commercial banks.

The inventory of real estate held by the RTC has received much attention. Little notice has been made of the properties of FDIC. However, you may find a diverse collection of properties available from the agency.

The FDIC generally markets properties through exclusive listings with local brokers. In addition, regional offices have sales staffs that will receive sealed bids for properties. From time to time, there may be auctions when enough properties exist to make one feasible. Prices and terms are negotiable. The FDIC can provide seller financing, if necessary. These interim loans have terms of 3 to 5 years with a long-term amortization schedule and a balloon payment requirement. For more information, see your broker or the closest sales office of FDIC. It will be listed in your phone directory under "Federal Deposit Insurance Corporation." Some directories print government agencies on colored paper in the front or rear of the book. If there is no listing in your local directory, try the nearest major city.

As the FDIC's inventory diminishes, there may be a policy change that will shift their inventory to another agency, or a plan to dispose of it themselves more quickly. Such a change could create brief but excellent opportunities for bargain hunters. Stay in touch with real estate publications and people in the real estate market to be informed of possible changes, not only for a change in FDIC policy, but for any matter.

21

BUYING FROM THE RESOLUTION TRUST CORPORATION

The Resolution Trust Corporation (RTC) was created by Congress in 1989 to take over the massive task of closing down insolvent savings and loan associations and liquidating property seized in these closures. The amount of real estate included in this inventory is valued at around $100 billion. Most is concentrated in the Southwest (particularly Texas, Oklahoma, and Arizona), but as real estate markets struggle in other parts of the nation, the inventory promises to become more extensive.

Since these properties were once financed and foreclosed upon by savings and loans, there are a lot of homes in the inventory. In many areas the RTC is by far the largest holder of foreclosed homes in the market. In addition, the agency has a strong mandate to sell these properties as an offset to the large costs of cleaning up the savings and loan mess.

On the other hand, there are some important problems with trying to buy from the RTC. First, the agency was created from scratch and has had its share of start-up difficulties. A major problem was just determining what it had to sell. Another was establishing procedures for accepting offers. Many early bidders report having a hard time just finding the right person to provide information on a property.

Originally, the RTC demanded bids no lower than 95 percent of market value, based on a recent appraisal. In addition, all transactions had to be for cash, with no concessions or seller assistance. The absence of bids has forced modification of these rules. At latest report, asking prices will be reduced by a set percentage and marked down again after another time period. Also, there are limited amounts of seller financing available. These policies are in transition and may be changing over time. Check with your local RTC sales office for the latest information. A list of RTC Sales Centers by region is provided in the Appendix.

A second difficulty for the general buyer or investor is the Affordable Housing Program instituted in 1990. This program sets aside the more modestly valued homes for sale to individuals who qualify for the program (based primarily on income). There are financing plans associated with the program, as well.

This program is a boon if you qualify and are looking for a home (check with your state's Housing Finance Agency for details), but it may limit severely the properties you can consider if you do not qualify.

In late 1991, the RTC introduced a newsletter, *Silver Lining*, so named because housing affordability was the silver lining in the dark cloud of the savings and loan crisis. You may get a copy of it by writing to the RTC, Affordable Housing Disposition Program, 801 17th Street, 6th Floor, Washington, D.C. 20434.

In many regions the RTC is an incredibly rich source of potential bargain homes. The availability may make it worthwhile to wade through the red tape and delay involved with a new government agency.

In addition to housing, the RTC offers a rich source of foreclosed commercial property, including hotels, office buildings, and shopping centers. When considering income-producing property, carefully estimate the rent and occupancy rate that exists and will likely continue. Subtract operating costs such as property taxes, insurance, maintenance, management, and repairs. Determine whether the remaining balance will be ample to pay interest and principal on any loan, and provide an adequate return on your proposed equity investment.

22

BUYING FROM FANNIE MAE

The Federal National Mortgage Association, also referred to as Fannie Mae or FNMA, was created by the federal government to help organize a secondary market in mortgage loans. This means FNMA buys loans that have been originated by others: mortgage bankers, banks and savings and loan associations. FNMA loans may be kept as investments or sold to investors in "pools." FNMA is a private organization owned by stockholders (though the U.S. government appoints some members to its board of directors). For the most part, FNMA operates as a private business.

Because FNMA owns loans, it often obtains properties when the loans are foreclosed. Like other owners of repossessed homes, the agency markets these properties to the public. The homes in inventory vary in value and quality. There is a limit to the amount of loan FNMA can acquire, but it is much larger than the limit on FHA loans. This means that FNMA will probably have some higher priced homes than the FHA. Mortgage limits are changed with the type of loan, geographic location, and are changed over time.

Most of the homes in the FNMA inventory are less than five years old. When necessary, the agency will remodel or repair the homes to make them more salable. However, some are offered as is.

The agency uses a variety of methods to sell homes. It contracts with local brokers to list properties. It may advertise homes in the local paper. Occasionally, auctions are held on a group of homes in an area. You may obtain a list of available homes in your area by calling a toll-free number (1-800-553-4636; in Maryland, 1-800-221-4636) or by writing to the main office (Fannie Mae Properties, PO Box 13165, Baltimore, MD 21203).

An asking price is set for all properties based on a professional appraisal and an opinion of probable selling price from a local broker. However, the agency is willing to negotiate a price with an interested buyer. In addition, the agency is willing to offer financing when necessary to complete a sale.

There are several advantages to working with FNMA. The agency is relatively free from bureaucratic requirements that slow down negotiations and final approval. It is fairly easy to get information and place a bid. Prices are negotiable and financing is available.

FNMA has less of a social welfare goal than does RTC or HUD. Consequently, investors are welcome to bid competitively with potential occupants. Investors may find themselves at a disadvantage in securing as much financing as owner-occupants.

23

PRE-FORECLOSURE SALES

Foreclosure is almost always a financial catastrophe for the homeowner and often presents the lender with a loss as well. Therefore, it is to everyone's interest to avoid the event. The homeowner will try to sell the home when facing difficulties in keeping up payments. However, if the sale will not yield enough money to pay off the loan, most financially strapped homeowners have little choice other than allowing foreclosure to proceed.

Knowing that foreclosure sales rarely cover the outstanding loan and expenses, lenders sometimes will try to work out a solution with a homeowner who wishes to keep the home and retains some ability to support a loan. Such a work-out may involve restructuring the loan to provide lower monthly payments or even accepting a reduced pay-back.

When a lender is willing to be flexible to revive a loan, there may be an opportunity for a third party, you, to forge an attractive deal. This is particularly the case when the present homeowner clearly has no ability or intention to retain the home. You may step into the homeowner's place and break the roadblock to working out a solution that avoids foreclosure.

Such situations will not be widespread, even when foreclosures are running at above-normal levels. Many loans are held in institutional pools that may preclude any type of work-out that lowers their value. In any case, you would need to step in before foreclosure had begun. The key to identifying such cases is a knowledgeable broker who works with homeowners and is aware of the possibilities of a pre-foreclosure sale. If you are interested in such opportunities, inform a broker you have confidence in that you might be willing to party to a work-out under the right terms. It will not be surprising if the broker has several current cases of homeowners faced with the likelihood of foreclosure. However, the broker must also be willing to contact the lender and sound out the possibilities of a work-out. Another source is classified ads in the newspaper where individuals may advertise for sale by owner (FSBO). Individual owners may also plant a "for sale" sign in their yard. It is worth a call to get more information and a feel for the market.

Before entering into negotiations, there are some bits of information you should gather. Of course you should inspect the property to see whether it is suitable for your lifestyle, just as in any other purchase. Determine your maximum price based on comparable properties and, if you intend to rent out the home, what price will be low enough to allow rent to provide a reasonable return. Make sure the loan that is being restructured is the only lien against the property. You do not want to be surprised by a bill for delinquent taxes or homeowner association dues or find out later that a second mortgage exists. Find out the terms on the existing loan and whether the lender can and will allow it to be assumed. If not, you may have to arrange outside financing. In most cases, the lender will prefer restructuring the financing if the price is right, since this may avoid the necessity of devaluing the loan on the lender's books.

A mutually beneficial match on a pre-foreclosure sale may be hard to find. However, when it does occur, it can be extremely beneficial. Think of yourself as providing the key to a win-win solution for both the lender and homeowner. But do it only if the deal also works to your benefit.

24

BUYING FROM A RELOCATION COMPANY

Homes held by relocation companies are not foreclosed homes, but offer opportunities to negotiate good bargains with highly motivated sellers. Furthermore, the fact that a relocation company is trying to sell a home, rather than its resident-owner, usually means that a buyer's market exists, and good prices should result.

Companies with offices or other facilities around the country periodically need to transfer employees from one location to another. This is particularly true of executive and technical personnel. Often these employees buy homes, even though they are aware of the possibilities of frequent relocation. When market conditions are good, selling these homes is no problem and often is an additional source of income for the homeowner. However, in slow markets, an employee may not be able to sell quickly without taking a sizable loss. Many companies assist employees by reimbursing losses or buying the home from the employee. There are firms that specialize in marketing these homes and they are often referred to as relocation companies.

When a relocation company takes over a home, it will usually refurbish the property, if needed, to make it more appealing to buyers. This generally means a new carpet and coat of paint. The property is put back on the market by listing it with a broker. Therefore, the way to find such homes is by contacting a broker who is a member of the local Multiple Listing Service (the MLS is a system that allows any member broker to sell any home in the system). Brokers frequently hang a "relocation company" sign on the "for sale" sign to make the buyer's motivation obvious to the market. It will also signal a message that the house is ready to be moved into, so there need not be any negotiation on the date of possession.

In most aspects, buying a home from a relocation company is just like buying from any other seller. However, the company may be more flexible, since the home is vacant and is costing the company money to hold. In most cases, the company should be amenable to reasonable offers. Do not expect to bargain for seller financing. On the other hand, the company may be willing to pay some closing costs. In addition, you will be able to include contingencies in the contract for financing, inspections, and other considerations. This is usually not possible when bidding on foreclosed homes.

Don't expect to buy one of these homes at a rock-bottom price. In most cases, these are quality homes and should command decent prices in all but completely devastated markets. Do expect to find a motivated seller who will work with you to try to reach an agreement.

25

FINDING PROPERTIES

The first step in buying repossessed real estate is to do a market search and find out what is available. In ordinary times, most properties are marketed through professional brokers, becoming part of the general inventory of listings. But when foreclosures are above normal, as in the late 1980s and early 1990s, a number of extraordinary methods are being used to market properties. Here are some of the sources of information you may want to look for:

Brokers. Many owners of REO still market property through brokerage firms, even though the inventory is large. In most cases, brokers operate under exclusive listings, which allow them to aggressively market the properties. The homes also become a part of the local Multiple Listing Service, which broadens the market.

Ads. Many properties are featured in classified ads in local newspapers. You can spot repossessed homes by the identification of the seller, such as "HUD homes" or an RTC ad. Such ads may have been placed by a broker or directly by the property owner. In most cases, a contact is provided for more information on the properties and bidding process.

Lists. HUD, FNMA, and RTC have compiled lists of properties. The lists usually provide only the basic information and no sales pitch such as may be found in classified ads. However, these lists cover a large number of properties and allow you to screen by price, location, or building type. For a list in your area, contact the owners of repossessed property identified in the appendix.

Auctions. Holders resort to auctions when inventories are large and the costs of holding the properties exceed the prospects of their value increasing. Professional auctioneers advertise several weeks before holding a sale. Look for such ads in local newspapers. Often sales brochures are available, listing the properties being sold.

Signs. Foreclosures and relocation company owned properties are frequently identified by "For Sale" signs planted in front yards. These are easily identified by walking or driving through the neighborhoods where you might wish to purchase a home.

Other methods. Accumulation of repossessed inventory has inspired some unusual techniques for getting rid of it. In New England, bankers have appeared at sales conventions in an effort to attract buyers of repossessed property. Special television shows have been devised to induce sales. In times of high foreclosures, any number of methods may be tried. Therefore, the interested buyer should keep alert for sources of information. At the same time, property buyers should be wary of bogus offers that appear to be too good to be true. They probably are. In any crisis situation, there are always those who will try to take advantage of people.

26

WORKING WITH A BROKER

Real estate markets are often hard to get a handle on. Most properties are different in some important ways that are not immediately apparent. The attractiveness, and thus value, of specific locations may vary over time. If you are not involved in the market frequently, you cannot gather the necessary information and keep it current for an informed decision.

Real estate brokers are involved in the market frequently and can be an excellent source of information. It makes sense to use their services when they can help you find the best deal. This is especially true when the service comes at no direct cost to you. (Some may argue that you are paying for this service whether you use it or not.)

Brokers can be very useful in finding properties. Many repossessed homes are sold like any other home, through exclusive listing contracts and even the Multiple Listing Service. The broker can provide access to this inventory. If the property is being sold by a government agency, a broker may assist you in making a bid, using the proper procedure and form. A broker may even represent you or accompany you to an auction.

Regardless of how helpful a broker is, you should keep in mind that he or she is an agent of the seller. The broker is employed by the seller to help arrange a sale. Brokers work with buyers because that is the way to induce sales. A broker is legally and ethically bound to provide you with accurate information about the property, but is not prevented from presenting it in its best light. Further, the broker is not allowed to provide personal information that would harm the seller, such as the seller's finances, marital status, or what the seller's lowest price would be. Instead of answering your question on what price the seller is likely to accept, the broker may suggest that you make an offer. The broker should not volunteer that the seller is anxious or desperate to sell because of relocation, divorce, or loss of a job as that has no bearing on the usefulness of the property. Nevertheless, a broker can be of assistance once you understand how the system works.

There is a growing movement under which some brokers offer to represent buyers. The so-called "buyers broker" may engage in activities that could be helpful to someone looking for a particular property. For example, you may hire a broker to find repossessed homes within a specified price range that offer seller financing. If you sign a contract with the broker, you may expect that the search will include all properties on the market, not just those for which the broker has a listing contract. Expect, as well, to have to pay for these services, either a commission based on the sale price or a fixed fee. Some buyer's brokers also take a commission from the seller, but taking a fee from both is frowned upon and, if done, must be open and disclosed to all parties or the broker will have violated rules or regulations of the state broker licensing agency.

27

INSPECTING THE PROPERTY

You should always inspect a property thoroughly before making an offer. When you are buying repossessed property, such an inspection is even more important, since it may be difficult or impossible to insert an addendum into the sales contract to cover repairs. In addition, many repossessed homes have sat vacant for extended periods (some may even have been vandalized by their previous owners) and may need repairs and remedial upkeep. You will want to know about such conditions before you bid because the condition of the property will affect how much you bid or even if you bid at all.

Since you are concerned about what a property is worth—even if the home is ideally suited to you, there is no need to bid more than market value—you should inspect the property from the viewpoint of an appraiser. This means you want to look at several different factors that affect the property's market value. The most logical way to approach this is to start with the more general and move to the specific. This also provides the advantage of allowing you to screen out properties without going through an entire analysis. In fact, at the more general levels, you can consider more than one property at a time.

Let's say that you want to invest locally and have settled on the general area. You should develop some idea of what neighborhoods are the most desirable for the type of property you want to own. You should check out the location from the standpoint of how convenient it is to employment centers and other areas of interest. This should be evaluated from the viewpoint of your lifestyle (if you plan to occupy the home) or that of your prospective tenants (if you plan to rent out the home). For example, access to public transportation may be important for college students or the elderly.

Next look at the residential quality of the neighborhood. Is it attractive? Is there too much traffic? Are there conveniently located parks? Do people maintain their homes well? Does the area appear to be changing in its use (encroaching commercial uses, vacant buildings, conversions of single-family homes to apartments)? The home you are considering may be in excellent condition. However, a deteriorating neighborhood will frustrate the best maintenance program and as an individual homeowner, there is little you can do about it.

Look at how the property fits into the neighborhood. Is there a great amount of conformity? Do surrounding homes have features that the subject lacks, or vice versa? In general, it is better to be deficient (and pay less) if the home can be brought up to the area standards without great expense. Adding features that are uncommon to the neighborhood will do little to improve the value of the home.

Finally, examine the home. You may want to employ a professional home inspector to help you at this stage. The inspector will check out the plumbing, mechanical, and electrical components of the home and point out any deficiencies and defects. You may need a second inspector, a structural engineer, for the foundation. A good inspector should be able to find things that may take you several years to discover. Make a list of things that can be repaired economically and things that would cost too much to do (such as changing an awkward floor layout). You can estimate the cost of doing the repairs and the reduced value of putting up with those features that cannot be changed.

This information will be helpful when you are preparing a bid (see Key 28). It may be that you can avoid bidding at all, if the property is not suitable or has too many problems. In fact, you may write off entire neighborhoods based on your initial evaluations.

28

MAKING AN OFFER

There are various procedures by which you can make an offer on repossessed property. One method popular with governmental agencies is the sealed bid (see Key 29), whereby you submit an offer with the terms kept a secret from other bidders. You bid at an auction too but then you know what others are bidding. Quite a bit of inventory can be bid on by making an offer through an agent and negotiating a contract just like any other piece of real estate.

The key to making an offer, regardless of the method, is setting a reservation price and sticking to it. A reservation price is the highest price you will pay for a property without paying more than it is worth to you (see Key 5). If market conditions are in your favor, you should be able to get the property for something less than your reservation price. Your first offer can be for much less than your maximum. The gap between this initial offer and the reservation price provides room to negotiate, if necessary.

Your reservation price is not necessarily market value. There may be features of the property that are especially valuable to you, or some that have no value. Therefore, everyone's maximum value is different. In a competitive bidding process, the winner will be the one who values the property highest. It is tempting to pursue a property when bidding starts. Remember, however, that unless the property is priceless to you, winning the bid at too high a price nullifies the whole point of buying repossessed property. After all, you are in this market to obtain a bargain.

To set your reservation price, you must know something about what is available in the current market and, preferably, what sold and for how much. Since you are an active buyer, this should not be too difficult. You may have information on asking prices (maybe even some sales data) for properties that are very similar to the one you are considering buying.

Note any differences in the properties that would affect their value to you. If the subject has some important feature that is lacking in the comparison property (appraisers call these "comparables"), add an amount to the asking price. If the subject is deficient in some feature, subtract an amount. How much to add or subtract? If the feature is something that could be added, adjust by the cost of making the addition. If not, you must judge how much you would be willing to pay to have the feature. Ignore items that you would not care about (or, if you will rent out the home, items that would not add to the rent you could charge).

Once you have a reservation price, you can devise a bidding strategy. If the procedure is sealed bid with no minimum limit on bid amounts, deduct about 10 percent from your reservation price and submit the amount. The amount of discount depends on how popular you think the property will be. If you have lost several bids previously on similar properties, you might bid your full reservation price. If the seller has set minimum bid amounts, compare them to your reservation prices. If they are too high, you might pass and wait for the property to come down in price. In an auction, your reservation price tells you when to stop bidding. Opening bids are usually mandated by the auctioneer.

In a normal negotiation between seller and buyer, you will go through several stages of offer and counter-offer. You can offer something substantially lower than your reservation price as an initial offer. Negotiations can continue until the seller agrees to your price or you reach your reservation limit.

If you are seeking seller financing, the terms of the loan should be factored into your maximum price. This can be done by calculating the monthly payments you would pay with market financing at your reservation price. This becomes the maximum monthly costs that you would be willing to bear to obtain the property.

29

BID SELECTION

There are various methods used to accept bids and select winners. This Key serves to explain some of the terms used to describe those methods.

A **sealed bid** process requires bidders to submit offers with no knowledge of competing bids. There may or may not be an asking price for the property (in some cases, an acceptable bid must be at or near the asking price). The bid should cover the entire transaction, including any requirement for seller payment of closing costs or seller-provided financing. Usually, such bids are collected over a short period when a listing is first released. This allows adequate time for all interested bidders to respond.

When the bids are opened, they are arranged in order of highest value. If there is a minimum bid price, any bids below the standard are eliminated. If the top bids are identical, the agency will select the winner on the basis of a set of priorities. Generally, cash bids are preferred to ones calling for financing. In some cases, there is a target group (such as someone who will occupy the home) that will receive favorable treatment.

The winning bidder is informed of the results of the selection process and given time to respond. Those who made unsuccessful bids receive their deposits back. A winning bidder who does not respond, will, in most cases, forfeit the deposit, though there are provisions for hardship cases. Procedures for choosing another bid vary. If the winner goes through with the purchase, the deposit is applied to the price.

Open bidding works much like any real estate transaction. The prospective buyer makes an initial offer in response to the seller's announcement of the availability of the property. The seller may accept the offer, reject the offer (cutting off negotiations), or respond with a counter-offer. The counter rejects the terms of the buyer's offer and suggests a new amount. A series of counter-offers from each side may continue until both sides agree or one party cuts off the negotiation. When an agreement is settled, the final contract of sale is signed and a closing date set.

Before placing a bid for property, obtain as much information as available about the bidding process and any procedures for inspecting the property. Note, particularly, any restrictions placed on bids and any reservations or priorities set for who can bid. In many cases, bids may be placed through a real estate agent approved by the selling agency. Finally, try to ascertain when the agency will announce the winning bid. You may find it not worthwhile if your bid is tied up in indecision for an extended period.

30

FINANCING

Most purchases of real estate require some type of financing. The mortgage lending industry in this country is well developed and is flexible enough to accommodate most borrowers' needs. However, getting a mortgage loan to buy repossessed property can be a problem.

A mortgage loan is secured by the real property purchased with the proceeds. In other words, the lender looks to the value of the property as protection in case the borrower defaults on the loan. That is why the lender requires a property description (survey) and appraisal of the property before approving the loan.

In many situations, if you buy repossessed property you need to have pre-arranged financing. That is because many sellers do not allow contingencies in the sales contract that would allow buyers to apply for a mortgage loan after the contract is signed. Such a contingency allows you to back out of the agreement and recover your earnest money deposit if the loan is not approved (in fact, most contingencies state the terms of the loan that must be obtained). If you know before bidding that financing will be approved, you can pursue the property with some assurance that a transaction will result and that your deposit will not be lost.

While a lender will not approve a loan without the collateral specified, it may be possible to get pre-qualified based on your financial position. The lender may run a credit check, verify your income and other financial resources, and specify the limit of your borrowing ability. You may even obtain a general description of the quality of property that could be financed through that institution. The lender may rule out condominiums or duplexes, for example. If you need FHA financing, you will want to know any restrictions that apply to the property to be financed. You will have the additional advantage of knowing how big a loan is possible, so you will know the most you can bid for a property.

Another option is to use your present home or some other property you currently own to secure the loan. This option offers the advantage of completely pre-arranged financing with no risk that the loan on new property will be turned down after you have committed to buy the property. The disadvantage is that you are putting additional property at risk should you be forced to default on the loan. Also, you need to have substantial equity built up in the properties to be able to mortgage them. This type of financing can be expensive, especially if the property already has a mortgage on it.

Seller-provided financing can be an advantage, even when the terms are similar to those available in the market. The financing goes with the sale and, therefore, you won't lose the transaction because financing cannot be arranged. Of course, most sellers who are willing to finance would really prefer cash. So if you are depending on seller financing, you are at a competitive disadvantage to cash bidders.

31

SHOULD YOU PARTICIPATE IN AUCTIONS?

When markets are slow and foreclosures abound, inevitably there will be a number of large real estate auctions. Holders of REO periodically turn to auctions to help clear their inventories. The auction process is a good way to attract a number of willing buyers and to assure sales of properties.

Should you, as an individual investor or homebuyer, participate in this process? You may think that bidding at an auction is for professionals who are savvy to the ways of auctioneers and that a novice may get lost in the flurry of activity at a typical bidding session. To some extent this is true. You do need to know something about the way auctions are conducted. However, it is even more important to know the property that you are bidding on and what its maximum value is to you. It is also important to exercise some self control so that you do not get carried away in the pursuit of a popular parcel.

But that doesn't mean you should avoid auctions. Indeed, some of the best bargains have been obtained at auctions, and by people with very little experience in buying real estate.

Auctions have long carried the stigma of property dumping. The general feeling is that if you can't sell a property through normal channels, you put it up for auction. Maybe this is a carry- over from the special auction used at foreclosure sales. However, public auctions are different. The method is commonly used for such commodities as art works and agricultural products, and these sales techniques often produce spectacular sale prices.

Generally, holders of real property resort to auctions because they think that the property will not increase in value over time and that waiting for a normal sale is not worth the carrying costs. To that extent, the properties offered may be had for bargain prices. However, knowledgeable sellers know that an auction may produce the highest price possible for a property. They are hoping that there will be enough bidding activity from motivated buyers to result in a sale at maximum value.

In reality, when a large number of properties are sold at auction, many do go for prices above their market value. At the same time, several sell for truly bargain prices. It depends on how much competition there is for each property.

For many properties, there is no way to tell how much they are worth. Their original sales price, in the case of previously owned properties, is no guide in a depressed market. You can make a determination, but it requires doing some homework: inspecting the property and checking with current sales of comparable properties. If you are willing to do this background checking, you will be prepared to bid intelligently for the properties you want.

Other Keys in this section will help you prepare. You will find information on how to find auction opportunities, how auctions work, how to prepare, and what you may end up with if you bid.

32

FINDING AUCTION OPPORTUNITIES

From a real estate marketing standpoint, auctions are major events. Unless foreclosures are especially heavy, auctions are not conducted frequently. Therefore, you will need to keep apprised of upcoming auctions and be prepared to act when they take place.

Auction companies know that attracting a sizable crowd is the key to generating high sales prices. Consequently, a lot of effort goes into promoting the event. Look for ads in the real estate section of the local newspaper. Call auction companies or institutions that hold REO (often the auctioneers are not local, especially if the area is not a large city). If an auction is planned, they should be able to provide you with a brochure or list of properties. These properties should be open for inspection prior to the sale.

In areas where a lot of inventory is sold by auction, special publications have developed to inform buyers of opportunities. These publications list properties that are for sale by owners who have acquired the property through foreclosure. You can subscribe to these services or purchase individual copies of the publications.

You may prefer to operate through a real estate broker. Often, brokers can earn commissions if someone they register at an auction buys a property. Advise your broker of your interest in property auctions and let him or her keep you informed of upcoming opportunities. The broker will probably make it easier to inspect properties before the sale.

33

HOW AN AUCTION WORKS

Once you decide to participate in an auction, you should understand how auctions are conducted. There are different types of auctions. They vary in the way bids are placed, in the way a winning bid is awarded, and in the scope of what is offered at auction. Almost all real estate auctions begin with a minimum bid suggested by the auctioneer. Bids from the audience are taken until no one is willing to outbid the last, highest bid. After a brief period, the property is awarded to the highest bidder. If no one is willing to bid the minimum price, the property may be re-entered at a lower starting point or may go unsold. When a large number of properties are offered at auction, the entire bidding process for each property may last only a few minutes.

An important consideration is whether any reservations are placed on the bidding process. An absolute auction awards the property to the highest bidder no matter what the winning bid is. In this way, the seller is assured the property will be sold (unless there are no bids at all), and the bidders are assured of getting the property at the winning bid price.

Some sellers are uncomfortable with the idea of selling at any price and may insist on a minimum bid. In this case, if no one places a bid at least as high as the minimum, the property will not be sold. This may happen when a seller is unsure of the market and is willing to hold the property if it does not bring a specified price. It may also be evidence that the seller does not completely trust the auction process, particularly when the turnout is lower than expected. (Sometimes a minimum is enforced by the courts in foreclosure sales to protect the defaulting borrower from abuse by the lender.)

The most restricted auctions are those with unstated reservation prices (Dutch or one-sided auctions). The seller can decide after the bidding whether or not to accept the highest bid. There is some question, when this tactic is used, as to whether the seller really wanted to sell or merely get a feel for the market value of the property. You may not want to participate in auctions where the highest bid can be turned down.

It is also instructive to know the scope of the auction. A stand-alone auction typically deals with only one property. This is rare, except in the case of foreclosure sales. Single-owner auctions are very common. Holders of REO or developers may conduct an auction covering all or a portion of their inventory. In general, these auctions do not employ reservations or minimum bids and the policies for bidding on each property are uniform. A multiple-owner auction may be used when several owners join together because their holdings are not large enough to justify individual auctions. In such auctions, there is a greater possibility that reservations will be placed on some properties.

In the end, your decision to participate in an auction will hinge on the quality of the properties included and any additional considerations included. For example, the seller may have arranged for financing to be offered on properties sold.

34

TIPS FOR BIDDING AT AN AUCTION

The key to getting an auction bargain is knowing the properties you are bidding on, having a reservation price for each property, and avoiding getting caught up in the bidding frenzy. These principles should prevent you from paying too high a price for a property you expected to be a bargain (the point of going to the auction in the first place).

Knowing the properties means actually investigating each property you are interested in. Prior to the sale, you can obtain a list of properties that will be sold. You should have an opportunity to visit the properties. You should spend the same effort you would if you were making an offer on the property through a negotiated sales contract. If the location and other features are desirable, you may even employ a professional inspector to check over the property. If the property is a condominium, you may want to look at the legal papers that affect what you can do within the unit and the common property.(Some condos may preclude leasing out units.)

Armed with the information you find in your investigations, you can form an opinion of the property's value. This will be the basis for your reservation price, the highest price you will bid at the auction. The opening bid, the original price, and any other value information obtained at the auction are not adequate guides to how much you should pay for the property. You must form your own idea of its value.

When the actual bidding opens, the auctioneer will usually set a starting bid. This bid is set at least 30–40 percent below the expected price for the property (or market value). The auctioneer will try to generate bidding enthusiasm by encouraging higher bids. There may be required increments by which the current bid must be raised. In some cases, it is possible to enter written bids before the auction starts. In this way, you can bid on property without having to be present at the auction. These bids are entered by the auctioneer and are valid until someone out-bids the entry. If no bids exceed the written bid, the submitter wins the property at a price one increment above the next highest bid.

When bidding is active, there is a tendency for the price to rise quickly. Unless you absolutely must have the property, you should stick to your reservation price even if it means losing out. Remember that your purpose is to get a bargain. The effect of active bidding in a good auction is what causes bid prices to be at or even higher than market value appraisals for many properties.

It is always possible that bidding will be tepid enough on some properties so that an uninformed bidder can end up with a good deal. However, when bidding is active, there is no substitute for adequate preparation. There are no good guidelines in the bidding process to tell you how much you should bid. You must know how much the property is worth to you. It is no disgrace (nor a waste of time) to go home empty-handed.

35

PAYING FOR YOUR AUCTION BUY

Being the winning bidder for the property you want is great, but you still have to finance the purchase. At the bottom of a market cycle, some buyers are able to buy so cheaply that they can pay cash or put the purchase on their credit cards. You are not likely to find such conditions very often. When you do, it may be because the property will require a lot of additional costs or will not produce income for some time.

Financing an auction purchase may be a bit more tricky than other purchases. You may need to pre-arrange credit before the auction. Most auctions allow a certain amount of time for buyers to line up their financing, recognizing that lenders require a specific piece of property to be identified before approving a loan. However, if your application is turned down, you will probably forfeit your deposit.

You should familiarize yourself with all regulations of the auction before hand. Many require bidders to have a cashiers check or certified check for at least $500 before allowing them to enter the bidding area. Winning bidders may need to come up with some percentage of the price shortly after the auction. Find out what is required for you to bid and how much time, if any, is provided for loan approval.

Some auction sellers offer financing as a way to attract more bidders. The loans are usually provided at favorable terms compared to the market, often with a low downpayment or no credit check. This is especially the case when the properties being offered are modestly priced homes. The sellers are hoping to attract home buyers. Seller financing makes the financing problem much less troublesome. Find out what is offered before attending. Factor any financing terms into your reservation price. You can afford to pay a higher price if financing is included at rates below market.

36

ELIGIBILITY FOR FMHA PROGRAMS

Key 18 described opportunities to purchase homes held by FmHA, the Farmers Home Administration (part of the federal Department of Agriculture). Significant benefits, as well as priority in bidding, are available for people who are eligible for the FmHA loan programs. The qualifications are the same as those applied to applicants for the various loan programs of FmHA.

The FmHA makes home loans in an attempt to offset the problems that rural homebuyers often encounter when looking for financing. Therefore, their loan programs seek to target people who need housing, yet have too little income to qualify for available loans from private sources. If you are buying for investment, or if you are looking for a mid-price house, you will not qualify for the program. If you have a good credit rating but a modest income and need a home, you may be eligible for the special treatment.

Formally, to be eligible, you must

- Be without decent, safe and sanitary housing
- Be unable to obtain a loan from private lenders on terms and conditions you can reasonably be expected to meet
- Have adequate and dependable income within FmHA income limits
- Possess the legal capacity to incur debt and have reached the legal age of majority
- Personally occupy the home on a permanent basis
- Have a credit history that indicates ability and willingness to meet obligations when they become due.

Income limits for the program are the same as those used by HUD, and are available from the local HUD office. These figures are changed annually to keep up with the median income of the targeted population. Adjustments to the income limits are made for the number of people in the household.

To see if your income falls within the guidelines of program eligibility, you need to obtain current program details and do some minor arithmetic. Add up the incomes of all adults in the household. Deduct a specific percentage from this total. Finally, deduct a specified dollar amount per minor living in the household. The result should fall within agency guidelines if you are eligible.

You can bid for an FmHA home even if you are not eligible to participate in their program. However, eligibility puts you in an especially favorable position to buy and to get financing through the agency. Such "program financing" may offer extended amortization terms, subsidized interest rates, and periods of payment moratoriums. However, eligible buyers are expected to move to non-program financing when they become qualified through increases in income or improvements in loan availability.

37

RTC AFFORDABLE HOUSING PROGRAM

When the Resolution Trust Corporation (RTC) was created to liquidate assets from failed savings and loan associations, Congress included a provision that created opportunities for moderate income homebuyers. This reflected a public concern for the plight of non-homeowners who were having trouble finding affordable housing. It seemed that, since the government had a surplus of homes to get rid of, this would be a good way to help solve the problem.

The RTC sells properties primarily through sealed bids (see Key 21). Under the affordable housing provision, homes valued at $67,500 or less are reserved for low- and moderate-income bidders for the first 90 days in which they are offered. A low-income person is one earning up to 80 percent of the area median income. A moderate-income person earns up to 115 percent of the median. Therefore, these guidelines include most people who would be in the market for homes in this price range. Other than the reservation, the bids are handled in the same manner as other bids submitted to the RTC.

In some parts of the country where large inventories of unsold homes exist (presently the Southwest), start-up problems have been reported with the program. Initially, most homes were not included in the reservation because the RTC's appraisals were too high. Of course, bidders could still compete to purchase the homes. However, bid prices had to be at least 95 percent of appraised value. The agency has since relaxed this provision. Also, it is experimenting with seller financing to assist sales. In most states, financing can be arranged through the state housing agency, which provides special low-interest loans to first-time homebuyers. Lining up an affordable home through the RTC program and a subsidized loan through the state program may prove tricky.

A bigger problem has been getting information on available homes before they are offered. Often, properties have been put out for bids before bidders could locate and inspect them, thereby reducing the number of eligible bids. As the agency works down its inventory and gathers experience, this problem should be minimized.

A parallel program offers the really hard-to-sell homes to non-profit and public agencies for free. These properties are generally in need of repair. The accepting agency may fix them up and offer them either for sale or as rental housing. Check with local housing program officials to see if any of these groups are operating in your area and what their requirements are.

38

URBAN HOMESTEADING

Lenders and those associated with the mortgage industry are not the only ones who acquire homes through the foreclosure process. The obligation to pay property taxes creates a lien on the taxed property. Occasionally, a property owner defaults on the taxes and the city must foreclose to enforce the obligation. Therefore, a municipality may have an inventory of homes that can be purchased.

It stands to reason that, if someone loses a property because of non-payment of back taxes, the property is probably not very valuable. Indeed, there may be major problems with the structure that will require substantial investment. The properties often become a public hazard as they sit unoccupied.

In a number of cities, programs have been initiated to find occupants for such homes. Generally, a person who qualifies can acquire a home for a nominal amount. Sometimes a token amount, such as $1, is required, and the government must create a lottery to give all those eligible a chance at being chosen. Such programs are an adaptation of the land give-aways that help populate much of the western United States in the nineteenth century.

The city's requirements are that the purchaser must agree to bring the property up to the city housing code and to personally occupy the home. Bringing a substandard dwelling up to code is often a challenging, expensive proposition to perform, especially as an evening or weekend task. You will have to rewire, replumb, and re-do just about everything in the house. Walls will have to be torn down to provide access to the wiring and plumbing. Supplies and tools are expensive. Even though you are willing to supply the sweat equity, you will have to put in more labor and effort than an experienced professional would. Still, urban homesteading programs are so popular that auctions are conducted to determine who gets the property.

If you are interested in getting a home through such a program (investors probably are not eligible for free homes), contact your city's housing office or community affairs office. They should be able to tell you about present or past programs in their city, and they may indicate whether to expect new programs. If there is an existing program, they will provide information for your participation and let you know what procedures are necessary.

39

SALES CONTRACTS

In most Northeastern states a *binder* is used to make an initial offer. When accepted, the owner agrees to take the property off the market and have an attorney prepare, in the next few days, a contract for the sale of the property.

In other parts of the country, a *sales contract* formalizes the negotiation process between you and the seller. This form is called a *contract of sale, agreement of sale,* or *earnest money contract* in different parts of the United States.

To make a binding offer, you must use a written contract. Contracts for the sale of real estate must be in writing to be enforceable. Besides, the seller can't respond in any meaningful way to a verbal offer because there are so many details to be arranged. If you are working through a broker or agent, he or she will have pre-printed standard contract forms. In some states the exact wording of the form is determined by the state agency that regulates professional real estate licenses, called the real estate commission. As an alternative, you could have an attorney draft a contract for you. However, the standard forms cover the most common items needed for the sale of a house.

You should realize that once you submit an offer in the form of a sales contract, the seller may accept your offer by signing the contract. The contract then becomes binding on both you and the seller. If the seller counter-offers, it will most likely be in the form of modifications to the contract you submitted. A counter-offer is legally a rejection of the offer and a substitution of a new offer. The counter-offer becomes binding when you initial all changes made. Negotiations become more difficult if you begin to add new requirements to the contract. Therefore, when you make your first offer, you should be careful to include all items you want in the contract.

If you have never seen a sales contract, this discussion

may be a little confusing. The contract states the price you are willing to pay for the home, but it also covers all conditions attached to the sale. Remember that the price is only one point in the negotiation of a sale. Agreement must be reached on how the price is met, timing of the sale, what is included in the sale, who pays selling and financing costs, the move-in dates, and under what conditions either party can back out of the sale.

All contracts identify the seller and buyer, the property involved, and the offered price. References to the property should include a legal description and identify what is to be included (any furnishings? mineral rights?). Price should be elaborated by stating the amount of cash down payment, money to be provided through a mortgage loan, and any money paid immediately as a deposit (earnest money).

The reason financing provisions are important is that most contracts include a contingency provision in case you are turned down for the loan. If you can't get the loan, this clause allows you to recover your earnest money. At the same time, it frees the seller to offer the home to another buyer. Generally, there are separate forms for conventional, FHA, and VA financing. The seller needs to know the type of financing, since some loans require the seller to pay discount points. The type of financing used may affect the price and other points of negotiation.

Other contingencies may be placed in the contract for the protection of the buyer. You probably want to condition the sale on the property successfully passing inspections for physical condition and absence of wood destroying insects, especially termites. These provisions give you the right to have the property inspected (at your expense). If anything is found wrong, the seller has the option of repairing the problem or, if too costly, releasing you from the contract. You may also require the right to void the sale if the property is found to be in a flood prone (hazard) area. If you own a home currently, you may make the sale contingent on selling your home. The seller may have the right to accept back-up contracts from other potential buyers. If the seller finds another buyer while the property is under contract to you subject to a contingency, you may be allowed 48 hours to delete the contingency and agree to close in coming days, or the seller will have the right to sell to the other party.

The contract sets a date for the closing and identifies who is responsible for the various expenses of sale. The latter provision is important if these expenses are not handled in the customary way. For example, if you want the seller to pay for discount points or if you are offering to pay the broker's commission, it should be stated in the contract. What is written in a contract is what matters. Verbal promises vanish into thin air. If you do not understand a provision in the contract at any point in the negotiation, ask your broker or attorney to explain it. Make sure the explanation fits_many brokers will not admit that they do not understand a provision in a pre-printed contract. Once signed, the contract will dictate how the sale is conducted and determine how much you pay and what you will get. No changes are allowed in the contract unless the other party agrees to them.

40

NEGOTIATION

One of the keys to buying real estate is good negotiation. In the United States most prices are set by the seller, but this is not the case for real estate. Consequently, participants in a real estate transaction are often unfamiliar and uncomfortable with the bargaining process. Of course, you could accept the other party's offer and complete the transaction quickly, but that would be to your financial detriment and regret.

When negotiating a price, both seller and buyer should have an idea of their *reservation prices*. This is the minimum price the seller will accept or the maximum price the buyer can pay. If you are the seller, your reservation price may be *market value*. You figure you can get this price on the market if the deal falls through. If you are the buyer, your reservation price will be *investment value*. This is how much the property is worth to you, considering your personal situation.

The seller will add a margin to his or her reservation price, while the buyer will subtract a margin to start the bargaining. This gives each party some bargaining room. Each hopes to get a better deal than the reservation price, if possible. Whether the seller or buyer has to come close to the reservation price depends on competition in the market. If there are lots of properties on the market, the buyer is in a good position and may extract concessions from the seller. If there are lots of buyers and few good properties, the seller can insist on the reservation price. You should be aware of the competitive condition of the market when negotiating.

Bargaining starts when the buyer makes an offer for the property. The seller may accept or reject this offer, but usually comes back with a counter offer at a higher price. The buyer then responds with another offer. The process continues until either both parties agree to terms or negotiations stop because of an impasse. Often in this process of offer and counter offer, terms of sale other than price come into play.

Either party may give in on price in return for concessions on other terms. In the process, you should keep in mind your reservation price (in terms of total costs) and try to move the negotiations toward the form of deal that best fits your situation.

Virtually everything in a property transaction is negotiable. This means not only the price but other terms such as:

- The form of payment (all cash at closing, deferred payments, other property)
- Who pays closing costs (the seller may pay the buyer's loan discount points, title policy premium, or other costs. The buyer may pay the seller's brokerage commission)
- Terms of financing, if the seller provides the loan (amount, interest rate, term of loan)
- Guarantees (the seller may guarantee a minimum rental income)
- Timing of closing (the buyer may wish to delay the closing to allow time to arrange financing or sign up tenants)
- Contingencies (sale subject to financing or sale of another property)

It is important to recognize that the total cost of the transaction is what counts, not merely the stated price. If you are willing to meet the seller's price, you may be able to get concessions on other items that may be more important. For example, the seller may be willing to finance the sale by lending a substantial amount of the cost. The interest rate and repayment terms then become crucial issues. Getting a lower interest rate on a long-term loan, even if only 1 percent lower, can be equivalent to a property price reduction of up to 10 percent.

When negotiating, you shouldn't feel that you are trying to take advantage of the other party. Recognize that offers contain margins for bargaining and your objective is to get the best deal possible. At the same time, you must be realistic in your demands and be willing to compromise if you really want to close the deal.

41

SELLER FINANCING AND PRICE

Sometimes a piece of real estate is offered with financing. In many cases, the terms are better than those possible from outside lenders, so this type of financing can be very advantageous. Not only does it make financing the purchase easier, but the terms offer considerable savings. Indeed, the financing may make the purchase a bargain even if you pay market value for the property.

Therefore, you should take the provision of favorable financing terms into consideration when determining your reservation price. Although terms on a loan and a lump sum price appear to be two different things, there are techniques for converting one to the other for comparison. In finance jargon, this is called "cash equivalence," and it is a valuable tool for finding the real price paid for a property.

In essence, when you buy a property with seller financing, you are buying two items: real property and financing terms. If the terms of the loan are the same as those on other loans in the market, the terms have no special value. What makes them valuable are the monthly savings you may enjoy during the financing period. These savings are the difference between what you would have paid with market financing and what you are actually paying as a result of the seller financing. You can convert these monthly savings into a lump sum value estimate of the savings today, called a "present value." Doing so requires a technique called "discounting," which simply means that a $1 dollar in savings today is more valuable than a $1 in savings later because of potential interest earnings. Consider it a discount on the price of the property. You can base the discount on the full loan term or a shorter period if you anticipate a sale or refinancing before the loan is fully paid off.

81

An accurate estimate of cash equivalence involves some rather detailed calculations which require a financial calculator or set of tables. However, in most cases, you will not need to be highly precise in your analysis. A general idea of the magnitude of savings possible is enough to reflect it in your reservation price. The table below has been worked out as an aid in the process.

The table is based on a market rate of interest of 10 percent. If the actual rate is more or less, it will not make a big difference. The numbers in the table are the approximate percent of discount from the asking price represented by the financing terms. In other words, you can afford to add that much more to the asking price in exchange for the financing terms. The rows refer to the percentage of the price that can be financed. The columns refer to how many percentage points the interest rate is below the market rate. Each column is divided into loans of 25 and 20 years.

For example, say a home is offered for $100,000. The seller will provide a loan of $75,000 (75 percent of the price) for 20 years at an interest rate one percentage point below the market. Looking at the 75 percent row and the column under one percentage point and 20 years, we find the discount to be 5 percent. A price of $105,000 (or 5 percent higher) with the financing terms is equivalent to paying $100,000 and financing with a market-rate loan.

The body of the table shows the increase in price to compensate for a below-market interest rate.

Percentage Points Below Market Interest Rate

| Loan/ | One Percent | | Two Percent | | Three Percent | |
Price	25 yrs	20 yrs	25 yrs	20 yrs	25 yrs	20 yrs
100%	7	7	15	13	22	20
75%	6	5	11	10	17	15
50%	4	4	7	7	11	10

42

CONDOMINIUM CONSIDERATIONS

A large part of the foreclosure market is in condominiums. There are hundreds of thousands of "condo slaves," people who bought condos at high prices and high interest rates who can't afford to absorb a loss from a sale and don't have the cash to refinance them. For example, a person may have bought a condo for $100,000 with a $90,000 loan at 15 percent. The property is now worth $60,000, and interest rates in the market are 10 percent. However, a new lender will only lend 80 percent of current value ($48,000) which means that the present owner must present $32,000 in cash to reduce the current loan to $48,000 before it can be refinanced at 10 percent or sold at market value. This may be impossible, so the present owner continues the existing terms, absorbing the loss in high payments as a preference to abandonment with a loss in credit rating.

There are opportunities to buy condos at distressed prices. Look carefully at the situation before buying, especially at resale opportunities. All real estate, especially condos, can be like a mousetrap—easy to get into, hard to get out of. There are also some lifestyle considerations.

The biggest difference between living in a single-family, detached home and a condo or co-op is the close proximity of your neighbors. When you live in a detached home, you have a buffer of lawn and maybe a fence between you and your neighbor. In a condo or co-op, this division is often no more than a common wall. In addition, once you are outside your unit, you are sharing space with the other residents. One of the most important considerations in buying a condo or co-op is deciding whether this type of living arrangement is suitable for you and your family.

Condo/co-op living does have certain advantages. Among them are:

Cost. Multi-family housing uses less land and is often more economical to build because of common structural components and other design features. Therefore, these units are generally less expensive than detached homes of similar size and quality. (Of course, condo/co-ops can be very expensive housing when placed in exclusive locations, such as Park Avenue in New York.) Lower priced units are good starter homes for first-time home buyers. Lower prices mean smaller loan amounts, making it easier for young families to qualify for a mortgage. Attached units may be less expensive to heat and cool because of the insulating effect of neighboring units.

Location. Because they take less land per unit, condo/co-ops can be developed on high-cost land within major cities. This appeals to people who like being closer to downtown job and entertainment centers. On the other hand, these locations may not be as residential in character as single-family neighborhoods. This is a judgment you must make based on your desired life style.

Low maintenance. A big attraction for some condo/co-op residents is the freedom from many of the routine household tasks. Things like lawn maintenance and outside repairs are generally the responsibility of the association or board. You pay for these services through your monthly fee, but this is often cheaper than contracting independently for these services.

Life style. Some complexes are specifically designed to promote certain life styles. There may be organized social functions for young single adults. Older single people may like the security of having neighbors close by. Elaborate common area facilities may be conducive to entertaining. However, most complexes are not amenable to residents with small children, pets, or those who like gardening.

There are also disadvantages to living in attached housing. This is why some people would not be happy living in a condo or co-op. If the following concerns bother you, you should consider an alternative to buying a condo/co-op.

Privacy. This is probably the biggest objection many people have to condos and co-ops. Good design can minimize this problem. Soundproofing in common walls and ceilings, private entryways (often associated with town house designs), and private patios and decks can reduce the intrusion of your neighbors. However, attached housing frequently involves some loss of freedom.

Control. Much of what you can do in your home is determined by the by-laws of the condo/co-op and majority rule of the owners association or corporation. If you cherish the independence that home ownership entails, you may not want to own a condo or co-op.

Status. In many parts of the United States, condos and co-ops are indistinguishable from rental apartments. Therefore, you may find that much of the status advantage normally attached to home ownership is lost when you own a condo or co-op. In some areas, mortgage financing for these units has been a problem. Lenders either are unfamiliar with condo/co-op ownership or feel that the units are not as marketable as, and therefore less valuable collateral than, detached homes. By contrast, a Manhattan condo or cooperative is fashionable.

Appreciation. Markets for condos have been less stable than those for detached homes. In some areas, builders have badly overestimated the market, and a surplus of condos exist. Then, too, if demand for condos increases, rental apartments can be converted quickly to increase the supply. This means your unit may not increase in value as rapidly as other types of housing.

Resale restrictions. For co-ops, the authority of the board to screen prospective tenants may complicate your ability to sell your unit for the best price. By contrast, condo sales may generally be effected without neighbors' approval.

43

INVESTMENT ANALYSIS

Investment analysis is deciding if a particular investment opportunity is right for you. This involves knowing what you want and being able to figure out which investment is likely to satisfy your goals. This requires several steps. First, you may determine your investment objectives and translate them into criteria. These criteria allow you to reject inappropriate investments and pick the best of those that are appropriate. Next, decide on the type of investment: real estate, stocks, bonds, precious metals, etc. This choice depends on current asset prices and how you expect them to change in the future. It also depends on how your present investment portfolio is composed and how much diversification you need.

After you have some idea of what you want, the next step is to screen the available opportunities to eliminate those that don't fit your criteria. You may seek an expert to help you decide what to consider. When you have a set of investment alternatives that generally fit your requirements, try to decide on the best one. This consists of projecting how the investment is likely to perform, considering the chance that something will go wrong, and comparing the projected return to those offered by other investment opportunities.

There are several ways to approach investment analysis for real estate. Some investors like to review all information. Others prefer to play a hunch as to what will work. Some like detailed projections. Others base their decision on inspection of the property and surrounding area. Some try to find properties that are undervalued in the market. Others emphasize negotiation to make a profitable deal. Many investors take a short-term perspective and look only at current performance. Others take a long-term viewpoint and look for value appreciation.

Regardless of the approach, you need a projection of investment return to make a decision. Since the return from real estate investments depends on future rent, operating expenses, financing, and tax considerations, by estimating these you can estimate how the property will perform. Projections may be the focus of the decision or may supplement other sources of information. The important thing to remember is that projections are only as good as the assumptions used to make them. Assuming rapid increases in rental rates and unrealistic appreciation rates can make any investment look good. It is best to take a conservative approach to the projection and let speculation about possible improved performance be a separate factor in the decision.

Short term analysis can be used to screen properties. The following indicators may be calculated quickly with a few bits of information that are based on current performance:

Gross rent multiplier. This is the total gross rent divided by the price of the property. The lower the number, the less you are paying for the gross income. For example, a property that sells for $100,000 and rents for $1,000 per month has a multiplier of 100. If all other things were equal (operating costs, future value expectations) that would be a bargain compared to a property that costs 125 times monthly rent.

Overall rate of return or **capitalization rate.** This is the net operating income (rent less operating expenses) divided by the value of the property. This measure is preferred to the gross rent multiplier because it accounts for operating expenses. Also, it offers a percentage rate, which is a customary way to express rate of return. For example, if a property rents for $1,000 per month and the owner is responsible for taxes and insurance that total $250 per month, the amount left is $750 per month. For 12 months that is $9,000, or a 9 percent return on a $100,000 investment, the overall rate of return. You should also provide a vacancy and collection allowance and detail all operating costs that the owner will bear. This example was kept simple by just indicating some likely expenses.

Cash-on-cash return or **equity dividend rate.** This is the cash flow divided by the required equity investment, and is especially useful when you know how the property will be financed. You may use before-tax or after-tax cash flow. If after-tax cash flow is used, you should adjust the returns on alternative types of investment for taxes to make a meaningful comparison.

Long-term analysis requires more information and assumptions because you are projecting several years into the future. If you are considering a property whose value is likely to increase or decrease in the near future, or if inflation is significant, long-term analysis is probably worthwhile.

Potential investors need to be reminded that most real estate is not a passive investment. Typically, the owner must manage the property or go to the effort of finding a property manager and giving instructions regarding management policies. The owner must then keep the manager accountable for property management, including investment results. Details of investment criteria and further explanation of real estate investment considerations are offered in Barron's *Keys to Investing in Real Estate.*

44

APPRAISALS

An appraisal is an expert opinion of value. An expert is someone with the competence and experience to do the type of analysis required. You can get opinions of value from sales agents, the owner, the tenant, or anyone familiar with the property. However, these opinions may not be very useful and probably won't be convincing as evidence of value. Usually, an appraisal expert has attained some type of designation through formal study and examination by a recognized body.

For example, the MAI and SRA designations are awarded by the Appraisal Institute to those who pass certain tests, prepare detailed sample reports called demonstrations, and complete years of appraisal experience. Other highly credible organizations that award appraisal designations include the National Society of Real Estate Appraisers, the American Society of Appraisers, the International Association of Assessing Officers, and the National Association of Independent Fee Appraisers. Designations from these associations assure that the appraiser understands the principles of appraisal and subscribes to a code of professional ethics. Soon most states will have some sort of licensing requirements for appraisers that will require some experience and passing an examination.

An opinion is a judgment supported by facts and logical analysis. The appraiser considers all available information that reflects on the value of the property. He or she follows a logical process to arrive at the opinion. The result is not merely a guess but a careful reading of the facts in the case. A good appraiser avoids interjecting personal bias into the opinion and tries to figure out how the market views the property.

Value should be qualified as well. There are different types of value. The majority of appraisals seek to find *market value*. This is what the property is worth to typical purchasers in a normal market. It is used as a standard in many applications. If you are interested in what the property is worth under your personal circumstances, an appraisal can be made for *investment value*. An appraiser should be able to give an opinion of value under any conditions, as long as they are spelled out at the outset.

Most appraisals are used for factual support. Lenders use them to show that a property is worth enough to serve as collateral for a loan. Appraisals may be used in condemnation cases to award compensation. They can be used to challenge property tax assessments or to back up an income tax return. They may be used in settling an estate.

Appraisals may be used as decision tools as well. You can get an appraisal to help decide how much to offer. They may serve to assist banks when trying to manage repossessed properties or to work out a troubled project.

An appraisal does not determine the market price—it is supposed to follow or reflect what is happening in the market. However, if the property under contract has been priced above the appraised value, a lender may not provide the necessary loan. Instead, the lender may suggest that the price be renegotiated to a lower amount. In doing so, the appraisal may in fact determine the market price, contradicting its purpose as stated above.

GLOSSARY

Many of the following terms were adapted from the *Real Estate Handbook* or the *Dictionary of Real Estate Terms*, copyright Barron's Educational Series, New York.

Absolute auction All properties are sold to the highest bidder; the seller has no reservation prices.

Acceleration Causing the full amount of a loan to be due upon default of certain provisions.

Acceptance Agreeing to take an offer; the acceptance of an offer constitutes a contract.

Acre Measure of land containing 43,560 square feet.

Ad valorem tax Tax based on the value of the property.

Addendum An attachment to a contract, often to describe required inspections or financing terms.

Adjustable-rate mortgage (ARM) Loan where the interest rate fluctuates according to another rate, as when the mortgage rate is adjusted annually based on the one-year Treasury bill rate, plus a 2 percent margin.

Agency Legal relationship between a principal and agent arising from a contract in which the principal engages the agent to perform certain acts on the principal's behalf.

Agent One who undertakes to transact some business or to manage some affair for another, with the authority of the latter.

Agreement of sale Written agreement between buyer and seller to transfer real estate at a future date. Includes all the conditions required for a sale.

Amortization Gradual process of reducing a debt in a systematic manner.

Appraisal An expert's opinion of the value of property arrived at with careful consideration of all available and relevant data.

Appreciation Increase in the value of property.

As is Present condition of property. The "as is" clause is likely to warn of a defect.

Assessed value Value against which a property tax is imposed. The assessed value is often lower than the market value due to state law, conservative tax district appraisals, and infrequent appraisals.

Assignment Method by which a right or contract is transferred from one person to another.

Assumable mortgage Loan that can be transferred to another party. The transferee assumes the debt, but the original borrower is not released from the debt without a novation.

Auction An announced event whereby property is sold to the highest bidder. See *Absolute auction, Dutch auction.*

Balloon mortgage Loan having a large final payment.

Balloon payment Large final payment on a debt.

Bid The amount one offers to pay for real estate.

Bill of sale Document used to transfer personal property. Often used in conjunction with a real estate transaction where appliances or furniture are sold also.

Binder Brief agreement, accompanied by a deposit, showing intent to follow with a formal contract.

Bridge loan Mortgage financing between the termination of one loan and the beginning of another.

Broker One who is licensed by a state to act for property owners in real estate transactions, within the scope of state law.

Building codes Regulations established by local governments describing the minimum structural requirements for buildings; includes foundation, roofing, plumbing, electrical, and other specifications for safety and sanitation.

Cap Maximum rate of change of the interest rate on an adjustable-rate mortgage. The mortgage may have an annual or lifetime ceiling.

Capital gain Gain on the sale of a capital asset. If long-term (generally over six months), capital gains are sometimes favorably taxed. A personal residence is a capital asset.

Caveat emptor "Let the buyer beware." An expression once used in real estate to put the burden of an undisclosed defect on the buyer. This concept has been eroded in most states.

Chattels Personal property.

Clear title Title that connotes ownership free from clouds; marketable title.

Closing Date when buyer and seller exchange money for property.

Closing costs Various fees and expenses payable by the seller and buyer at the time of a real estate closing (also termed *Transaction costs*). Included are brokerage commissions, discount points, title insurance and examination, deed recording fees, and appraisal fees.

Closing statement Accounting of funds from a real estate sale, made to both the seller and the buyer separately. Most states require the broker to furnish accurate closing statements to all parties to the transaction.

Cloud on title Outstanding claim or encumbrance that, if valid, would affect or impair the owner's title. Compare *Clear title*.

Commission 1. Amount earned by a real estate broker for his services. 2. Official state agency that enforces real estate licensing laws.

Commitment letter Written pledge or promise; a firm agreement, often used to describe the terms of a mortgage loan that is being offered.

Common elements In a condominium, those portions of the property not owned individually by unit owners but in which an indivisible interest is held by all unit owners. Generally includes the grounds, parking areas, maintenance areas, recreational facilities, and external structure of the building.

Community property Property accumulated through joint efforts of husband and wife and owned by them in equal shares. This doctrine of ownership now exists in Arizona, California, Idaho, Louisiana, Nevada, New Mexico, Texas, and Washington State.

Comparables Properties that are similar to the one being sold or appraised. Used in the market approach to appraisal.

Competitive market analysis An estimate of what a property might bring based on the sale or offering of similar properties, usually by a real estate salesperson. Contrast *Appraisal*.

Conditional offer One that requires certain condition(s) to be fulfilled, such as rezoning of the property or the buyer's need to sell another property, before the contract is binding.

Conditional sales contract   Written agreement for the sale of property stating that the seller retains title until the conditions of the contract have been fulfilled. See *Contract for deed*.

Condominium   System of ownership of individual units in a multi-unit structure, combined with joint ownership of commonly used property (sidewalks, hallways, stairs, etc.). See *Common elements*.

Consideration   Anything of value given to induce entering into a contract; it may be money, personal services, or love and affection.

Contingency   Condition that must be satisfied before the party to a contract must purchase or sell. For example, financing is the most frequent contingency. A buyer who cannot arrange an appropriate loan need not complete the transaction and should receive a refund of the earnest money.

Contract   Agreement between competent parties to do or not to do certain things for a consideration. Common real estate contracts are contract of sale, contract for deed, mortgage, lease, listing, deed.

Contract for deed   Real estate installment sales arrangement whereby the buyer may use, occupy, and enjoy land, but no deed is given by the seller (so no title passes) until all or a specified part of the sale price has been paid. Same as *Land contract*, *Installment land contract*, *Conditional sales contract*.

Contract of sale   Same as *Agreement of sale*.

Conventional loan, mortgage   1. Mortgage loan other than one guaranteed by the Veterans Administration or insured by the Federal Housing Administration. See *VA loan, FHA loan*. 2. Fixed-rate, fixed-term mortgage loan.

Cooperative   Type of corporate ownership of real property whereby stockholders of the corporation are entitled to use a certain dwelling unit or other units of space. Special income tax laws allow the tenant stockholders to deduct interest and property taxes paid by the corporation.

Curtesy   Right of a husband to all or part of his deceased wife's realty regardless of the provisions of her will. Exists in only a few states.

Deed   Written document, properly signed and delivered, that conveys title to real property. See *General warranty deed, Quitclaim deed, Special warranty deed.*

Deed of trust   Instrument used in many states in lieu of a mortgage. Legal title to the property is vested in one or more trustees to secure the repayment of the loan.

Deed restriction   Clause in a deed that limits the use of land.

Default   Failure to fulfill an obligation or promise or to perform specified acts.

Deficiency judgment   Court order stating that the borrower still owes money when the security for a loan does not entirely satisfy a defaulted debt.

Department of Housing and Urban Development (HUD) U.S. government agency established to implement certain federal housing and community development programs.

Depreciation   1. In accounting, allocating the cost of an asset over its estimated useful life. 2. In appraisal, a charge against the reproduction cost (new) of an asset for the estimated wear and obsolescence. Depreciation may be physical, functional, or economic.

Discount points   Amounts paid to the lender (often by the seller) at the time of origination of a loan, to account for the difference between the market interest rate and the lower face rate of the note.

Dower   Under common law, the legal right of a wife or child to part of a deceased husband or father's property. Compare *Curtesy.*

Down payment   Amount one pays for property in addition to the debt incurred.

Due-on-sale clause   Provision in a mortgage that states that the loan is due upon the sale of the property.

Dutch auction   The seller has a reservation price but does not disclose it. If no bid exceeds the reservation price, the property will not be sold.

Earnest money   Deposit made before closing by a purchaser of real estate to evidence good faith.

Easement   Right, privilege, or interest that one party has in the land of another. The most common easements are for utility lines.

Encroachment   Building, a part of a building, or an

obstruction that physically intrudes upon, overlaps, or trespasses upon the property of another.

Encumbrance Any right to or interest in land that affects its value. Includes outstanding mortgage loans, unpaid taxes, easements, and deed restrictions.

Equity Interest or value that the owner has in real estate over and above the liens against it.

Equity loan Usually a second mortgage whereby the property owner borrows against the house, based on the value of equity built up by appreciation.

Equity of redemption The right of a borrower to regain property generally after default, before foreclosure.

Escrow Agreement between two or more parties providing that certain instruments or property be placed with a third party for safekeeping, pending the fulfillment or performance of some act or condition.

Et ux. Abbreviation of the Latin *et uxor*, which means "and wife."

Exclusive agency listing Employment contract giving only one broker, for a specified time, the right to sell the property and also allowing the owner alone to sell the property without paying a commission.

Exclusive right to sell listing Employment contract giving the broker the right to collect a commission if the property is sold by anyone, including the owner, during the term of the agreement. See *Multiple listing service*.

Execute To sign a contract; sometimes, to perform a contract fully.

Fair market value A term generally used in property tax and condemnation legislation, meaning the market value of a property.

Fannie Mae See *Federal National Mortgage Association*.

Federal Fair Housing Law Federal law that forbids discrimination on the basis of race, color, sex, religion, or national origin in the selling or renting of homes and apartments.

Federal Housing Administration (FHA) Agency within the United States Department of Housing and Urban Development that administers many loan programs, loan guarantee programs, and loan insurance programs designed to make more housing available.

Federal National Mortgage Association (FNMA) Corporation that specializes in buying mortgage loans, mostly from mortgage bankers. It adds liquidity to the mortgage market. Nicknamed Fannie Mae, FNMA is owned by its stockholders, who elect 10 of its board of directors. The United States president appoints the other five directors.

Fee simple or fee absolute Absolute ownership of real property; the owner is entitled to the entire property with unconditional power of disposition during his life, and it descends to his heirs and legal representatives upon his death intestate.

FHA loan Mortgage loan insured by the FHA.

First mortgage Mortgage that has priority as a lien over all other mortgages. In cases of foreclosure, the first mortgage will be satisfied before other mortgages.

Fixed-rate mortgage Loan on which the interest rate does not change over the entire term of the loan.

Fixtures Personal property attached to the land or improvements so as to become part of the real estate.

Foreclosure Termination of all rights of a mortgagor or the grantee in the property covered by the mortgage.

General warranty deed Deed in which the grantor agrees to protect the grantee against any other claim to title to the property and provides other promises.

Graduated-payment mortgage (GPM) Loan requiring lower payments in early years than in later years. Payments increase in steps each year until the installments are sufficient to amortize the loan.

Grantee Party to whom the title to real property is conveyed; the buyer.

Grantor Anyone who gives a deed.

Gross rent multiplier (GRM) Sales price divided by the rental rate.

Growing equity mortgage (GEM) Mortgage loan in which the payment is increased by a specific amount each year, with the additional payment amount applied to principal retirement. As a result of the added principal retirement, the maturity of the loan is significantly shorter than a comparable level-payment mortgage.

Hazard insurance A form of insurance that protects

against certain risks, such as fires and storms.

Homeowners' association   Organization of the homeowners in a particular subdivision, planned unit development, or condominium; generally for the purpose of enforcing deed restrictions or managing the common elements of the development.

Homeowner's policy   Insurance policy designed especially for homeowners. Usually protects the owner from losses caused by most common disasters, theft, and liability. Coverage and costs vary widely.

HUD   Department of Housing and Urban Development.

HUD home   One that was foreclosed and offered for sale by HUD.

Inside lot   In a subdivision, a lot surrounded on each side by other lots, as opposed to a corner lot, which has road frontage on at least two sides.

Joint tenancy   Ownership of real estate by two or more persons, each of whom has an undivided interest with the right of survivorship.

Junior mortgage   Loan whose claim against the property will be satisfied only after prior mortgages have been repaid. See *First mortgage, Second mortgage.*

Land contract   Same as *Contract for deed.*

Lien   Charge against property making it security for the payment of a debt, judgment, mortgage, or taxes; it is a type of encumbrance. A specific lien is against certain property only. A general lien is against all the property owned by the debtor.

List   To give or obtain a listing.

Listing   1. Written engagement contract between a principal and an agent, authorizing the agent to perform services for the principal involving the latter's property.   2. Record of property for sale by a broker who has been authorized by the owner to sell.   3. Property so listed.

Listing agreement, listing contract   Same as *Listing* (1).

Loan-to-value ratio (LTV)   Amount borrowed as a percentage of the cost or value of the property purchased.

Lot and block number   Method of locating a parcel of land. The description refers to a map of a subdivision that numbers each lot and block.

Market value Theoretical highest price a buyer, willing but not compelled to buy, would pay, and the lowest price a seller, willing but not compelled to sell, would accept.

Mechanic's lien Lien given by law upon a building or other improvement upon land, and upon the land itself, as security for the payment for labor done and materials furnished for improvement.

Mortgage Written instrument that creates a lien upon real estate as security for the payment of a specified debt.

Mortgagee One who holds a lien on property or title to property, as security for a debt; the lender.

Mortgagor One who pledges property as security for a loan; the borrower.

Mortgage banker One who originates, sells, and services mortgage loans. Most loans are insured or guaranteed by a government agency or private mortgage insurer.

Mortgage insurance Protection for the lender in the event of default, usually covering 10 to 20 percent of the amount borrowed.

Multiple listing service (MLS) Association of real estate brokers that agrees to share listings with one another. The listing broker and the selling broker share the commission. The MLS usually distributes a book with all listings to its members, updating the book frequently. Prospective buyers benefit from the ability to select from among many homes listed by any member broker.

National Association of Real Estate Brokers (NAREB) Organization of minority real estate salespersons and brokers who are called *REALTISTS*®.

National Association of *REALTORS*® (NAR) Organization of *REALTORS*®, devoted to encouraging professionalism in real estate activities. There are over 600,000 members of NAR, 50 state associations, and several affiliates.

Negative amortization Increase in the outstanding balance of a loan resulting from the failure of periodic debt service payments to cover required interest charged on the loan.

Net listing Listing in which the broker's commission is the excess of the sales price over an agreed-upon (net) price to the seller; illegal in some states.

Notary public Officer who is authorized to take acknowledgments to certain types of documents, such as deeds, contracts, and mortgages, and before whom affidavits may be sworn.

Novation Agreement whereby a lender substitutes one party to a contract for another, releasing the original party from any obligation.

Offer Expression of willingness to purchase a property at a specified price.

Open house Method of showing a home for sale whereby the home is open for inspection on an advertised date.

Open housing Condition under which housing units may be purchased or leased without regard for racial, ethnic, color, or religious characteristics of the buyers or tenants.

Open listing Listing given to any number of brokers without liability to compensate any except the one who first secures a buyer who is ready, willing, and able to meet the terms of the listing or secures the seller's acceptance of another offer. The sale of the property automatically terminates all open listings.

Oral contract Unwritten agreement. With few exceptions, oral agreements for the sale or use of real estate are unenforceable. In most states, contracts for the sale or rental of real estate, unless they are in writing, are unenforceable under the Statute of Frauds. Oral leases for a year or less are often acceptable.

ORE, OREO See *REO*.

Performance bond Assures that a contractor will perform in accordance with the contract and protects against a breach of contract.

Permanent mortgage Mortgage for a long period of time (over 10 years).

Plat Plan or map of a specific land area.

Points See *Discount points*.

Prepayment penalty Penalty imposed on a borrower when a loan is retired before maturity.

Prepayment privilege Right of a borrower to retire a loan before maturity.

Principal 1. One who owns or will use property.   2. One who contracts for the services of an agent or broker; the broker's or agent's client.   3. The amount of money raised by a mortgage or other loan, as distinct from the interest paid on it.

Principal and interest payment (P&I)   Periodic payment, usually made monthly, that includes the interest charges for the period plus an amount applied to amortization of the principal balance. Commonly used with self-amortizing loans.

Principal, interest, taxes, and insurance (PITI)   Monthly mortgage payment (P&I), with the addition of an amount deposited in escrow for future payment of taxes and insurance.

Private mortgage insurance (PMI)   See *Mortgage insurance.*

Prorate   To allocate between seller and buyer their proportionate shares of an obligation paid or due; for example, to prorate real estate taxes.

Purchase-money mortgage   Mortgage given by a grantee (buyer) to a grantor (seller) in part payment of the purchase price of real estate.

Quitclaim deed   Deed that conveys only the grantor's rights or interest in real estate, without stating the nature of the rights and with no warranties of ownership. Often used to remove a possible cloud on the title. Contrast with *General warranty deed.*

Real estate   1. In law, land and everything more or less attached to it. Ownership below to the center of the earth and above to the heavens. Distinguished from *personal property.* Same as *realty.*   2. In business, the activities concerned with ownership and use transfers of the physical property.

Real Estate Settlement Procedures Act (RESPA)   Law that states how mortgage lenders must treat those who apply for federally related real estate loans on property with one to four dwelling units. Intended to provide borrowers with more knowledge when they comparison shop for mortgage money.

REALTIST®   Member of the National Association of Real Estate Brokers, a group composed primarily of minority brokers.

REALTOR®   A professional in real estate who subscribes to a strict Code of Ethics as a member of the local and state boards and of the National Association of REALTORS®.

Redlining   Illegal practice of refusing to originate mortgage loans in certain neighborhoods on the basis of race or ethnic composition.

Refinance   To substitute a new loan for an old one, often in order to borrow more or to reduce the interest rate.

REO Real estate owned; also, other real estate (ORE). Refers to real estate owned by banks that is not used for banking operations.

Repossession Commonly used to mean the same as foreclosure; property claimed by lender for violation of a loan provision, usually non-payment.

Reservation price A mental note of the minimum a seller will accept; the maximum a buyer will pay.

Sales contract Same as *Contract of sale*.

Sealed bids Offers submitted in a closed envelope so that other bidders do not see what others are willing to pay.

Secondary mortgage market The "marketplace" where existing mortgages, mostly first mortgages on homes, are traded.

Self-amortizing mortgage Loan that will retire itself through regular principal and interest payments. Contrast with *Balloon mortgage*.

Seller's market Economic conditions that favor sellers, reflecting rising prices and market activity.

Settlement Same as *Closing*.

Special assessment Assessment made against a property to pay for a public improvement by which the assessed property is supposed to be especially benefited.

Special warranty deed Deed in which the grantor limits the title warranty given to the grantee to anyone claiming by, from, through, or under him, the grantor. The grantor does not warrant against title defects arising from conditions that existed before he owned the property. Often this type of deed is quite satisfactory. For example, a buyer in a foreclosure sale will receive a sheriff's deed, which is a special warranty against claims arising prior to foreclosure.

Specific performance Legal action in which the court requires a party to a contract to perform the terms of the contract when he has refused to fulfill his obligations. Used in real estate, since each parcel of land is unique.

Statutory According to statutes; pertaining to written laws.

Statutory redemption The right of a borrower to regain property that was foreclosed, according to written law.

Subcontractor One who performs services under contract

to a general contractor.

Subdivision   Tract of land divided into lots or plots suitable for home-building purposes. Some states and localities require that a subdivision plot be recorded.

Subject to mortgage   Arrangement whereby a buyer takes title to mortgaged real property but is not personally responsible for the payment of any portion of the amount due. The buyer must make payments in order to keep the property; however, if he fails to do so, only his equity in that property is lost.

Survey   Process by which a parcel of land is measured and its area ascertained; also, the blueprint showing the measurements, boundaries, and area.

Sweat equity   Value added to a property due to improvements as a result of work performed personally by the owner.

Term amortization   For a loan, the period of time during which principal and interest payments must be made; generally, the time needed to amortize the loan fully.

Terms   Provisions in a contract; interest rate and payment requirements of a loan.

Title   Evidence that the owner of land is in lawful possession thereof; evidence of ownership.

Title insurance   Insurance policy that protects the holder from loss sustained by defects in the title.

Title search   Examination of the public records to determine the ownership and encumbrances affecting real property.

Veterans Administration (VA)   Government agency that provides certain services to discharged servicemen.

VA loan (mortgage)   Loan that is guaranteed by the Veterans Administration. Discharged servicemen with more than 120 days of active duty are generally eligible for a VA loan, which typically does not require a down payment.

Vendee   Buyer.

Vendor   Seller.

Warranty deed   Title to real estate in which the grantor guarantees title. Usually protects against other claimants, liens, or encumbrances and offers good title.

Zoning ordinance   Act of city, county, or other authorities specifying the type of use to which property may be put in specific areas. Examples: residential, commercial, industrial.

CHECKLISTS

A good checklist is a useful device to try to ensure that nothing has been overlooked. Although a perfect home has yet to be built, a checklist may help determine whether a house has so many negatives that it is unsuitable for you, or has a "fatal flaw"— something you wouldn't want to own at any price. Use the list to help jog your memory about each feature.

General Checklist

Address
Date shown
Shown by
Owner's name
Phone number
Reason for selling
Availability or Urgency of sale
Age
Price
Special financing
    Assumption, seller
Loan status:
    Delinquent
    Default
    Foreclosed by:
        Local institution
        HUD
        VA
        Private mortgage insurer
Relocation company ownership
Taxes
Builder
Style, stories, or levels
Construction quality
Comments

Location Characteristics

	Superior	Average	Inferior
School district			
Elementary			
Junior high			
High			
Parochial			
Fire and police protection			
Transportation			
Medical facilities			
Shopping			
Recreational			
Religious facilities			
Neighborhood			
Subdivision			
Homeowner association			
View			

Interior Arrangements

	Superior	Average	Inferior
Number of bedrooms			
Closet(s) size, shelving			
Number of bathrooms			
Size, fixtures, floor			
Living room			
Family room			
Laundry/utility room			
Floor plan			
Floor coverings			
Window treatments			
Built-in cabinets			
Paint			
Wallpaper			
Fireplace			
Basement			
Additional Comments			

House Exterior— Quality or Condition

	Superior	Average	Inferior
Roof			
Facade			
Windows			
Drainage			
Paint			
Garage (size, attached)			
Attic			
Storage			
Additional Comments			

Lot

	Superior	Average	Inferior
Size, shape			
Fence			
Shrubbery			
Trees			
Lawn			
Sprinklers			
Swimming pool			
Patio			
Driveway			
Traffic			
Zoning			
Flood plain			
Environmental hazards			
Additional Comments			

Servicing

	Superior	Average	Inferior
Waste (Sewer, septic)			
Heating			
Air conditioning			
Insulation			
Ceiling			
Walls			
Weather-stripping			
Storm windows, doors			
Wiring			
Plumbing			
Appliances			
Additional Comments			

Negotiating

Asking price
Probable price
Financing
Points
Closing costs
   Legal
   Recording
   Appraisal
Inspections
   Inside
   Outside
   Pests
Contingencies
   Sale of old house
   Mortgage approval
   Mortgage terms
Additional Comments

Financing

Existing financing
   Assumability
   Lender(s), account numbers, phone numbers
   Unpaid balance(s), interest rate, remaining term, balloons
   Transfer fees
   Prepayment penalty
New Financing

Lender name and phone	Type (Fixed, Adj)	Rate	L-T-V	Term	Points	Fees	Lock-in	Other

Legal Considerations

Deed type
Homestead exemption
Spouse's name
Ownership form
   (joint tenancy, community property)
Title policy or abstract
Exceptions on title policy
Attorney's opinion of title
Additional Comments

PAYMENT TABLES

To calculate monthly payment requirements from tables on following pages:

1. Find intersection of Contract Interest Rate with Term (Years).
2. Multiply amount in table by thousands borrowed to result in monthly principal and interest payment.
3. Add estimated taxes and insurance (not shown on table).

Example: Find the monthly payment on a $90,000 loan for 25 years at $9\frac{1}{2}$ percent interest.

Step 1. 8.74 (read from table).
Step 2. Multiply by 90.
Result $786.60 is the monthly principal and interest payment.
Step 3. Add monthly tax and insurance requirement.

Monthly Principal and Interest Payments per $1,000 of Principal

Term	Contract Interest Rate (%)			
(Years)	6.00	6.25	6.50	6.75
1	86.07	86.18	86.30	86.41
2	44.32	44.43	44.55	44.66
3	30.42	30.54	30.65	30.76
4	23.49	23.60	23.71	23.83
5	19.33	19.45	19.57	19.68
6	16.57	16.69	16.81	16.93
7	14.61	14.73	14.85	14.97
8	13.14	13.26	13.39	13.51
9	12.01	12.13	12.25	12.38
10	11.10	11.23	11.35	11.48
11	10.37	10.49	10.62	10.75
12	9.76	9.89	10.02	10.15
13	9.25	9.38	9.51	9.65
14	8.81	8.95	9.08	9.22
15	8.44	8.57	8.71	8.85
16	8.11	8.25	8.39	8.53
17	7.83	7.97	8.11	8.25
18	7.58	7.72	7.87	8.01
19	7.36	7.50	7.65	7.79
20	7.16	7.31	7.46	7.60
21	6.99	7.14	7.28	7.43
22	6.83	6.98	7.13	7.28
23	6.69	6.84	6.99	7.14
24	6.56	6.71	6.87	7.02
25	6.44	6.60	6.75	6.91
26	6.34	6.49	6.65	6.81
27	6.24	6.40	6.56	6.72
28	6.15	6.31	6.47	6.63
29	6.07	6.23	6.39	6.56
30	6.00	6.16	6.32	6.49

Monthly Principal and Interest Payments
per $1,000 of Principal

Term (Years)	Contract Interest Rate (%)			
	7.00	7.25	7.50	7.75
1	86.53	86.64	86.76	86.87
2	44.77	44.89	45.00	45.11
3	30.88	30.99	31.11	31.22
4	23.95	24.06	24.18	24.30
5	19.80	19.92	20.04	20.16
6	17.05	17.17	17.29	17.41
7	15.09	15.22	15.34	15.46
8	13.63	13.76	13.88	14.01
9	12.51	12.63	12.76	12.89
10	11.61	11.74	11.87	12.00
11	10.88	11.02	11.15	11.28
12	10.28	10.42	10.55	10.69
13	9.78	9.92	10.05	10.19
14	9.35	9.49	9.63	9.77
15	8.99	9.13	9.27	9.41
16	8.67	8.81	8.96	9.10
17	8.40	8.54	8.69	8.83
18	8.16	8.30	8.45	8.60
19	7.94	8.09	8.24	8.39
20	7.75	7.90	8.06	8.21
21	7.58	7.74	7.89	8.05
22	7.43	7.59	7.75	7.90
23	7.30	7.46	7.61	7.77
24	7.18	7.34	7.50	7.66
25	7.07	7.23	7.39	7.55
26	6.97	7.13	7.29	7.46
27	6.88	7.04	7.21	7.37
28	6.80	6.96	7.13	7.30
29	6.72	6.89	7.06	7.23
30	6.65	6.82	6.99	7.16

Monthly Principal and Interest Payments
per $1,000 of Principal

Term	Contract Interest Rate (%)			
(Years)	8.00	8.25	8.50	8.75
1	86.99	87.10	87.22	87.34
2	45.23	45.34	45.46	45.57
3	31.34	31.45	31.57	31.68
4	24.41	24.53	24.65	24.77
5	20.28	20.40	20.52	20.64
6	17.53	17.66	17.78	17.90
7	15.59	15.71	15.84	15.96
8	14.14	14.26	14.39	14.52
9	13.02	13.15	13.28	13.41
10	12.13	12.27	12.40	12.53
11	11.42	11.55	11.69	11.82
12	10.82	10.96	11.10	11.24
13	10.33	10.47	10.61	10.75
14	9.91	10.06	10.20	10.34
15	9.56	9.70	9.85	9.99
16	9.25	9.40	9.54	9.69
17	8.98	9.13	9.28	9.43
18	8.75	8.90	9.05	9.21
19	8.55	8.70	8.85	9.01
20	8.36	8.52	8.68	8.84
21	8.20	8.36	8.52	8.68
22	8.06	8.22	8.38	8.55
23	7.93	8.10	8.26	8.43
24	7.82	7.98	8.15	8.32
25	7.72	7.88	8.05	8.22
26	7.63	7.79	7.96	8.13
27	7.54	7.71	7.88	8.06
28	7.47	7.64	7.81	7.99
29	7.40	7.57	7.75	7.92
30	7.34	7.51	7.69	7.87

Monthly Principal and Interest Payments per $1,000 of Principal

Term (Years)	Contract Interest Rate (%)			
	9.00	**9.25**	**9.50**	**9.75**
1	87.45	87.57	87.68	87.80
2	45.68	45.80	45.91	46.03
3	31.80	31.92	32.03	32.15
4	24.88	25.00	25.12	25.24
5	20.76	20.88	21.00	21.12
6	18.03	18.15	18.27	18.40
7	16.09	16.22	16.34	16.47
8	14.65	14.78	14.91	15.04
9	13.54	13.68	13.81	13.94
10	12.67	12.80	12.94	13.08
11	11.96	12.10	12.24	12.38
12	11.38	11.52	11.66	11.81
13	10.90	11.04	11.19	11.33
14	10.49	10.64	10.78	10.93
15	10.14	10.29	10.44	10.59
16	9.85	10.00	10.15	10.30
17	9.59	9.74	9.90	10.05
18	9.36	9.52	9.68	9.84
19	9.17	9.33	9.49	9.65
20	9.00	9.16	9.32	9.49
21	8.85	9.01	9.17	9.34
22	8.71	8.88	9.04	9.21
23	8.59	8.76	8.93	9.10
24	8.49	8.66	8.83	9.00
25	8.39	8.56	8.74	8.91
26	8.31	8.48	8.66	8.83
27	8.23	8.41	8.58	8.76
28	8.16	8.34	8.52	8.70
29	8.10	8.28	8.46	8.64
30	8.05	8.23	8.41	8.59

Monthly Principal and Interest Payments per $1,000 of Principal

Term (Years)	Contract Interest Rate (%)			
	10.00	10.25	10.50	10.75
1	87.92	88.03	88.15	88.27
2	46.15	46.26	46.38	46.49
3	32.27	32.38	32.50	32.62
4	25.36	25.48	25.60	25.72
5	21.25	21.37	21.49	21.62
6	18.53	18.65	18.78	18.91
7	16.60	16.73	16.86	16.99
8	15.17	15.31	15.44	15.57
9	14.08	14.21	14.35	14.49
10	13.22	13.35	13.49	13.63
11	12.52	12.66	12.80	12.95
12	11.95	12.10	12.24	12.39
13	11.48	11.63	11.78	11.92
14	11.08	11.23	11.38	11.54
15	10.75	10.90	11.05	11.21
16	10.46	10.62	10.77	10.93
17	10.21	10.37	10.53	10.69
18	10.00	10.16	10.32	10.49
19	9.81	9.98	10.14	10.31
20	9.65	9.82	9.98	10.15
21	9.51	9.68	9.85	10.02
22	9.38	9.55	9.73	9.90
23	9.27	9.44	9.62	9.79
24	9.17	9.35	9.52	9.70
25	9.09	9.26	9.44	9.62
26	9.01	9.19	9.37	9.55
27	8.94	9.12	9.30	9.49
28	8.88	9.06	9.25	9.43
29	8.82	9.01	9.19	9.38
30	8.78	8.96	9.15	9.33

Monthly Principal and Interest Payments per $1,000 of Principal

Term (Years)	Contract Interest Rate (%)			
	11.00	11.25	11.50	11.75
1	88.38	88.50	88.62	88.73
2	46.61	46.72	46.84	46.96
3	32.74	32.86	32.98	33.10
4	25.85	25.97	26.09	26.21
5	21.74	21.87	21.99	22.12
6	19.03	19.16	19.29	19.42
7	17.12	17.25	17.39	17.52
8	15.71	15.84	15.98	16.12
9	14.63	14.76	14.90	15.04
10	13.77	13.92	14.06	14.20
11	13.09	13.24	13.38	13.53
12	12.54	12.68	12.83	12.98
13	12.08	12.23	12.38	12.53
14	11.69	11.85	12.00	12.16
15	11.37	11.52	11.68	11.84
16	11.09	11.25	11.41	11.57
17	10.85	11.02	11.18	11.35
18	10.65	10.82	10.98	11.15
19	10.47	10.64	10.81	10.98
20	10.32	10.49	10.66	10.84
21	10.19	10.36	10.54	10.71
22	10.07	10.25	10.42	10.60
23	9.97	10.15	10.33	10.51
24	9.88	10.06	10.24	10.42
25	9.80	9.98	10.16	10.35
26	9.73	9.91	10.10	10.28
27	9.67	9.85	10.04	10.23
28	9.61	9.80	9.99	10.18
29	9.57	9.75	9.94	10.13
30	9.52	9.71	9.90	10.09

Monthly Principal and Interest Payments
per $1,000 of Principal

Term (Years)	Contract Interest Rate (%) 12.00	12.25	12.50	12.75
1	88.85	88.97	89.08	89.20
2	47.07	47.19	47.31	47.42
3	33.21	33.33	33.45	33.57
4	26.33	26.46	26.58	26.70
5	22.24	22.37	22.50	22.63
6	19.55	19.68	19.81	19.94
7	17.65	17.79	17.92	18.06
8	16.25	16.39	16.53	16.67
9	15.18	15.33	15.47	15.61
10	14.35	14.49	14.64	14.78
11	13.68	13.83	13.98	14.13
12	13.13	13.29	13.44	13.59
13	12.69	12.84	13.00	13.15
14	12.31	12.47	12.63	12.79
15	12.00	12.16	12.33	12.49
16	11.74	11.90	12.07	12.23
17	11.51	11.68	11.85	12.02
18	11.32	11.49	11.66	11.83
19	11.15	11.33	11.50	11.67
20	11.01	11.19	11.36	11.54
21	10.89	11.06	11.24	11.42
22	10.78	10.96	11.14	11.32
23	10.69	10.87	11.05	11.23
24	10.60	10.79	10.97	11.16
25	10.53	10.72	10.90	11.09
26	10.47	10.66	10.84	11.03
27	10.41	10.60	10.79	10.98
28	10.37	10.56	10.75	10.94
29	10.32	10.52	10.71	10.90
30	10.29	10.48	10.67	10.87

Monthly Principal and Interest Payments
per $1,000 of Principal

Term	Contract Interest Rate (%)			
(Years)	13.00	13.25	13.50	13.75
1	89.32	89.43	89.55	89.67
2	47.54	47.66	47.78	47.90
3	33.69	33.81	33.94	34.06
4	26.83	26.95	27.08	27.20
5	22.75	22.88	23.01	23.14
6	20.07	20.21	20.34	20.47
7	18.19	18.33	18.46	18.60
8	16.81	16.95	17.09	17.23
9	15.75	15.90	16.04	16.19
10	14.93	15.08	15.23	15.38
11	14.28	14.43	14.58	14.73
12	13.75	13.90	14.06	14.21
13	13.31	13.47	13.63	13.79
14	12.95	13.11	13.28	13.44
15	12.65	12.82	12.98	13.15
16	12.40	12.57	12.74	12.91
17	12.19	12.36	12.53	12.70
18	12.00	12.18	12.35	12.53
19	11.85	12.03	12.20	12.38
20	11.72	11.89	12.07	12.25
21	11.60	11.78	11.96	12.15
22	11.50	11.69	11.87	12.05
23	11.42	11.60	11.79	11.97
24	11.34	11.53	11.72	11.91
25	11.28	11.47	11.66	11.85
26	11.22	11.41	11.60	11.80
27	11.17	11.37	11.56	11.75
28	11.13	11.32	11.52	11.71
29	11.09	11.29	11.48	11.68
30	11.06	11.26	11.45	11.65

SALES OFFICES

RTC CONSOLIDATED OFFICES

RTC WESTERN REGION
Intermountain Consolidated Office
1515 Arapahoe, Tower III, Suite 800
Denver, Colorado 80202
Director: Keith Carson — 303-556-6500
800-542-6135

Sales Center
Director: Mike Cunningham — 303-556-6678

Coastal Consolidated Office
1901 Newport Boulevard
Costa Mesa, CA 92627
Director: James G. Klingensmith — 714-631-8600
800-283-9288

Sales Center
Director: Micah Leslie — 714-631-8600

Central Western Consolidated Office
2910 North 44th Street
Phoenix, Arizona 85018
Director: Dewey Porter — 602-224-1776
800-937-7782

Sales Center
Director: Richard Sinagoga — 602-224-1799

RTC SOUTHWESTERN REGION
Metroplex Consolidated Office
3500 Maple Avenue
Dallas, Texas 75219
Director: Jim Messec — 214-443-2300
800-782-4674

Sales Center
Director: Steven Hilts 214-443-4673

Southern Consolidated Office
Bexar Savings Association
10100 Reunion Place
San Antonio, Texas 78216
Director: James Forrestal 512-524-4700
800-388-4254

Sales Center
Director: Billie Colbert 512-524-4700

Gulf Coast Consolidated Office
2223 West Loop South
Houston, Texas 77024
Director: John Lomax 713-685-3400
800-879-8492

Sales Center
Director: David Franklin 713-888-2734

Austin Consolidated Office
4303 Victory Drive, Suite 201
Austin, Texas 78704
Director: Juan Patlan 512-443-9464
800-677-3044

RTC CENTRAL REGION
North Central Consolidated Office
3400 Yankee Drive
Eagan, Minnesota 55122
Director: Bob Fish 612-683-0036
800-873-5815

Sales Center
Director: Jerry Clerk 612-683-4601

Mid-Central Consolidated Office
4900 Main Street, Suite 200
Kansas City, Missouri 64112 816-531-2212
800-365-3342

Sales Center
Director: Dennis Cavinaw 816-531-2212

Lake Central Consolidated Office
25 Northwest Point Boulevard
Elk Grove, Illinois 60007
Director: Joe Minniti 708-806-7750
800-284-6197

Sales Center
Director: Donna Walker 708-290-7555

Northern Consolidated Office
4606 S. Garnett
Tulsa, Oklahoma 74146
Director: Virginia Kingsley 918-627-9000
800-759-3342

Sales Center
Director: Burton McNeil 918-587-7600

Bayou Consolidated Office
100 St. James, Building H
Baton Rouge, Louisiana 70802
Director: Don Wickens 504-339-1000
800-477-8790

Sales Center
Director: Julian Hecker 504-339-1375

RTC EASTERN REGION
Mid-Atlantic Consolidated Office
245 Peachtree Center Ave, N.W.
Atlanta, Georgia 30303
Director: William Dudley 404-881-4840
800-234-3342

Sales Center
Director: Phillip Jones 404-225-5798

Northeast Consolidated Office
1000 Adams Avenue
Norristown, Pennsylvania 19403
Director: Stephen Wood 215-650-8500
800-782-6326

Sales Center
Director: Herb Korte   215-631-4819

Southeast Consolidated Office
Freedom Federal Savings Assoc.
220 E. Madison Street, Suite 302
Tampa, Florida 33602
Director: Jimmy Caldwell   813-870-7000
                                    800-777-8777
Sales Center   813-870-7200

STATE HOUSING FINANCE AGENCIES SERVING AS RTC CLEARINGHOUSES

Alaska State Housing Authority
Mark Romick, Resource Development Analyst
(907) 562-2813

Arizona Department of Commerce
Office of Housing Development
Martina Kuehl
Housing Program Analyst
(602) 280-1365

Arkansas Development Finance Authority
C.E. Anderson
Vice President of Housing
(501) 682-5900

Colorado Housing & Finance Authority
David Martinez, Communications Director
(303) 297-7342

Connecticut Housing Finance Authority
Michael Ward, Program Planning Mgr.
(203) 721-9501

District of Columbia Housing Finance Agency
Michael V. Hodge, Affordable Housing Liaison
(202) 832-6604

Florida Housing Finance Agency
Florida Department of Community Affairs
Dave Mahlert, Planner
(904) 488-4197

Georgia Residential Finance Authority
David Crum, Program Director
(404) 679-4840

Illinois Housing Development Authority
Greg Lewis
Manager, Single Family Portfolio Admin.
(312) 836-5344
For Property Information: 1-800-472-0572

Iowa Finance Authority
Ted Chapler, Executive Director
(515) 242-4990

Kentucky Housing Corporation
Cheryl Harp, Director
Home Ownership Program
(502) 564-7630

Louisiana Housing Finance Agency
For Property Information
(504) 295-8450/8463

Maine State Housing Authority
Susan Guild, Director of Research
(207) 626-4600   1-800-452-4668

Maryland Community Development Administration
Tonna Phelps, Manager
Nonprofit Development Activities
(301) 514-7446

Massachusetts Housing Finance Agency
Rufus Phillips, Research & Program Development Officer
(617) 451-3480

Michigan State Housing Development Authority
Robert G. Brown, Director
Home Improvement Programs
(517) 373-8370

Minnesota Housing Finance Agency
Donna Dimatteo
Housing Program Technician
(612) 296-7608/797-3132

Mississippi Home Corporation
William Martin, Director of Programs
(601) 354-6062

Nebraska Investment Finance Authority
Susan Brunn, Housing Assistant
(402) 434-3911

Nevada Dept. of Commerce Housing Division
Mamie Chinn, Deputy Administrator
(702) 687-4258

New Hampshire Housing Finance Authority
Dean Christon, Deputy Exec. Director
(603) 472-8623

New Jersey Housing & Mortgage Finance Agency
Hotline, 1-800-NJ-HOUSE

New Mexico Mortgage Finance Authority
Michael Miller, Management Support Technician
(505) 843-6880

New York State Division of Housing & Community Renewal
Eileen Murray, RTC Program Manager
(518) 486-5085

North Carolina Housing Finance Agency
Tim West, Housing Officer
(919) 781-6115

Oklahoma Housing Finance Agency
Nancy Mount-English, Technical Advisor
(405) 840-4666

Oregon Housing and Community Services
Rebecca Hohn, CDC Secretary
(503) 378-5959

Pennsylvania Housing Finance Agency
Roy Newsome, Special Assistant to the Executive Director
(717) 780-3800

South Carolina Housing Authority
Chuck D. Hancock, Policy Officer
(803) 734-8702

South Dakota Housing Development Authority
Michael Echols, Executive Director
(605) 773-3181

Tennessee Housing Development Agency
Rebecca T. Garland, General Counsel
(615) 741-2400

Utah Housing Finance Agency
William Erikson, Executive Director
(801) 521-6950

Vermont Housing Finance Agency
Doug Lothrop, Director of Communications
(802) 864-5743

Virginia Housing Development Authority
Donald L. Ritenour, Director
Single Family
(804) 782-1986

Washington State Housing Trust Fund
Department of Community Development
Jeff Robinson, Housing Finance Unit Manager
(206) 753-6652

West Virginia Housing Development Fund
Steve Fisher, Deputy Chief, SF Loans
Servicing and Property Administration
(304) 345-6475

Wisconsin Housing & Economic Development Authority
Arlene Scalzo, Housing Officer
(608) 267-3806

Wyoming Commerce Development Authority
Cheryl Gillum, Subsidized Housing Program Officer
(307) 265-0603

HUD

Region I (Boston)
Boston Regional Office
Thomas P. O'Neil, Jr.
Federal Building, Room 375
10 Causeway Street
Boston, MA 02222-1092
(617) 565-5234

Hartford
330 Main Street, First Floor
Hartford, CT 06106-1860
(203) 240-4523

Manchester
Norris Cotton Federal Building
275 Chestnut Street
Manchester, NH 03101-2487
(603) 666-7681

Providence
330 John O. Pastore Federal Building and U.S. Post Office
Kennedy Plaza
Providence, RI 02903-1785
(401) 528-5351

Bangor
Casco Northern Bank Building, First Floor
23 Main Street
Bangor, ME 04401-4318
(207) 945-0467

Burlington
Federal Building, Room B-311
11 Elmwood Avenue
Post Office Box 1104
Burlington, VT 05402-1104
(802) 951-6290

Region II (New York)
New York Regional Office
26 Federal Plaza
New York, NY 10278-0068
(212) 264-8053

Albany
Leo W. O'Brien Federal Building
N. Pearl Street and Clinton Avenue
Albany, NY 12207-2395
(518) 472-3567

Buffalo
Statler Building, Mezzanine
107 Delaware Avenue
Buffalo, NY 14202-2986
(716) 846-5755

Camden
The Parkade Building
519 Federal Street
Camden, NJ 08103-9998
(609) 757-5081

Caribbean
159 Carlos Chardon Avenue
San Juan, PR 00918-1804
(809) 753-4201

Newark
Military Park Building
60 Park Place
Newark, NJ 07102-5504
(201) 877-1662

Region III (Philadelphia)
Philadelphia Regional Office
Liberty Square Building
105 South Seventh Street
Philadelphia, PA 19106-3392
(215) 597-2560

Baltimore
The Equitable Building, Third Floor
10 North Calvert Street
Baltimore, MD 21202-1865
(301) 962-2520

Charleston
405 Capitol Street, Suite 708
Charleston, WV 25301-1795
(304) 347-7036

Pittsburgh
412 Old Post Office Courthouse
7th and Grant Streets
Pittsburgh, PA 15219-1906
(412) 644-6388

Richmond
701 East Franklin Street
Richmond, VA 23219-2591
(804) 771-2721

Washington, DC
451 Seventh Street, SW, Room 3158
Washington, DC 20410-5500
(202) 453-4500

Wilmington
J. Caleb Boggs Federal Building, Room 1304
844 King Street
Wilmington, DE 19801-3519
(302) 573-6300

Region IV (Atlanta)
Atlanta Regional Office
Richard B. Russell Federal Building
75 Spring Street, SW
Atlanta, GA 30303-3388
(404) 331-5136

Birmingham
Daniel Building
15 South 20th Street
Birmingham, AL 35233-2096
(205) 731-1617

Columbia
Strom Thurmond Federal Building
1835-45 Assembly Street
Columbia, SC 29201-2480
(803) 765-5592

Coral Gables
Gables 1 Tower
1320 South Dixie Highway
Coral Gables, FL 33146-2911
(305) 662-4500

Greensboro
415 North Edgeworth Street
Greensboro, NC 27401-2107
(919) 333-5363

Jackson
Doctor A. H. McCoy Federal Building
Suite 910
100 West Capital Street
Jackson, MS 39269-1096
(601) 965-4738

Jacksonville
325 West Adams Street
Jacksonville, FL 32202-4303
(904) 791-2626

Knoxville
John J. Duncan Federal Building, Third Floor
710 Locust Street
Knoxville, TN 37902-2526
(615) 549-9384

Louisville
601 West Broadway
Post Office Box 1044
Louisville, KY 40201-1044
(502) 582-5251

Memphis
One Memphis Place, Suite 1200
200 Jefferson Avenue
Memphis, TN 38103-2335
(901) 521-3367

Nashville
251 Cumberland Bend Drive, Suite 200
Nashville, TN 37228-1803
(615) 736-5213

Orlando
Langley Building, Suite 270
3751 Maguire Boulevard
Orlando, FL 32803-3032
(407) 648-6441

Tampa
700 Twiggs Street
Room 527
Post Office Box 172910
Tampa, FL 33672-2910
(813) 228-2501

Region V (Chicago)
Chicago Regional Offices
300 South Wacker Drive
Chicago, IL 60606-6765
(312) 353-5680

547 West Jackson Boulevard
Chicago, IL 60606-5760
(312) 353-7660

Cincinnati
Federal Office Building, Room 9002
550 Main Street
Cincinnati, OH 45202-3253
(513) 684-2884

Cleveland
One Playhouse Square, Room 420
1375 Euclid Avenue
Cleveland, OH 44115-1832
(216) 522-4065

Columbus
200 North High Street
Columbus, OH 43215-2499
(614) 469-7345

Detroit
Patrick J. McNamera Federal Building
477 Michigan Avenue
Detroit, MI 48226-2592
(313) 226-6280

Flint
Gil Sabuco Building, Room 200
352 South Saginaw Street
Flint, MI 48502-1953
(313) 766-5109

Grand Rapids
2922 Fuller Avenue, NE
Grand Rapids, MI 49505-3409
(616) 456-2182

Indianapolis
151 North Delaware Street
Indianapolis, IN 46204-2526
(317) 269-6303

Milwaukee
Henry S. Reuss Federal Plaza
Suite 1380
310 West Wisconsin Avenue
Milwaukee, WI 53203-2289
(414) 291-3214

Minneapolis-St. Paul
220 Second Street, South
Minneapolis, MN 55401-2195
(612) 370-3000

Springfield
Lincoln Tower Plaza, Suite 672
524 South 2nd Street
Springfield, IL 62701-1774
(217) 492-4085

Region VI (Fort Worth)
Fort Worth Regional Office
1600 Throckmorton
Post Office Box 2905
Fort Worth, TX 76113-2905
(817) 885-5401

Albuquerque
625 Truman Street, NE
Albuquerque, NM 87110-6443
(505) 262-6463

Dallas
525 Griffin Street
Room 106
Dallas, TX 75202-5007
(214) 767-8300

Houston
Norfolk Tower, Suite 200
2211 Norfolk
Houston, TX 77098-4096
(713) 653-3274

Little Rock
Lafayette Building, Suite 200
523 Louisiana Street
Little Rock, AR 72201-3707
(501) 378-5401

Lubbock
Federal Office Building
1205 Texas Avenue
Lubbock, TX 79401-4093
(806) 743-7265

New Orleans
Fisk Federal Building
1661 Canal Street
New Orleans, LA 70112-2887
(504) 589-7200

Oklahoma City
Murrah Federal Building
200 NW Fifth Street
Oklahoma, OK 73102-3202
(405) 231-4891

San Antonio
Washington Square
800 Dolorosa
San Antonio, TX 78207-4563
(512) 229-6806

Shreveport
New Federal Building
500 Fannin Street
Shreveport, LA 71101-3077
(318) 226-5385

Tulsa
Robert S. Kerr Building, Room 200
440 South Houston Avenue
Tulsa, OK 74127-8923
(918) 581-7435

Region VII (Kansas City)
Kansas City Regional Office
Professional Building
1103 Grand Avenue
Kansas City, MO 64106-2496
(816) 374-6432

Des Moines
Federal Building, Room 259
210 Walnut Street
Des Moines, IA 50309-2155
(515) 284-4512

Omaha
Braiker/Brandeis Building
210 South 16th Street
Omaha, NE 68102-1622
(402) 221-3703

St. Louis
210 North Tucker Boulevard
St. Louis, MO 63101-1997
(314) 425-4761

Topeka
Frank Carlson Federal Building, Room 370
444 S.E. Quincy
Topeka, KS 66683-0001
(913) 295-2652

Region VIII (Denver)
Denver Regional Office
Executive Tower Building
1405 Curtis Street
Denver, CO 80202-2349
(303) 844-4513

Casper
4225 Federal Office Building
100 East B Street
Post Office Box 580
Casper, WY 82602-1918
(307) 261-5252

Fargo
Federal Building
653 2nd Avenue North
Post Office Box 2483
Fargo, ND 58108-2483
(701) 239-5136

Helena
Federal Office Building, Room 340
Drawer 10095
301 South Park
Helena, MT 59626-0095
(406) 449-5205

Salt Lake City
324 South State Street
Suite 220
Salt Lake City, UT 84111-2321
(801) 524-5237

Sioux Falls
"300" Building, Suite 116
300 North Dakota Avenue
Sioux Falls, SD 57102-0311
(605) 330-4223

Region IX (San Francisco)
San Francisco Regional Office
Phillip Burton Federal Building
  and U.S. Courthouse
450 Golden Gate Avenue
Post Office Box 36003
San Francisco, CA 94102-3448
(415) 556-4752

Indian Programs Office, Region IX
1 North First Street, Suite 400
Phoenix, AZ 85004-2360
(602) 261-4156

Fresno
1603 E. Shaw Avenue
Suite 138
Fresno, CA 93710-8193
(209) 487-5036

Honolulu
Prince Jonah Federal Building
300 Ala Moana Boulevard
Post Office Box 50007
Honolulu, HI 96850-4991
(808) 541-1343

Las Vegas
1500 E. Tropicana Avenue
Suite 205
Las Vegas, NV 89119-6516
(702) 388-6500

Los Angeles
1615 W. Olympic Boulevard
Los Angeles, CA 90015-3801
(213) 251-7122

Phoenix
1 North First Street, Third Floor
Post Office Box 13468
Phoenix, AZ 85002-3468
(602) 261-4434

Reno
1050 Bible Way
Post Office Box 4700
Reno, NV 89505-4700
(702) 784-5356

Sacramento
777 12th Street
Suite 200
Sacramento, CA 95814-1997
(916) 551-1351

San Diego
Federal Office Building, Room 5-S-3
880 Front Street
San Diego, CA 92188-0100
(619) 557-5310

Santa Ana
34 Civic Center Plaza
Box 12850
Santa Ana, CA 92712-2850
(714) 836-2451

Tucson
100 North Stone Avenue
Suite 410
Tucson, AZ 85701-1467
(602) 629-5220

Region X (Seattle)
Seattle Regional Office
Arcade Plaza Building
1321 Second Avenue
Seattle, WA 98101-2054
(206) 442-5414

Anchorage
701 "C" Street
Box 64
Anchorage, AK 99513-0001
(907) 271-4170

Boise
Federal Building, U.S. Courthouse
550 West Fort Street
Post Office Box 042
Boise, ID 83724-0420
(208) 334-1990

Portland
520 Southwest Sixth Avenue
Portland, OR 97204-1596
(503) 221-2561

Spokane
West 920 Riverside Avenue
Spokane, WA 99201-1075
(509) 456-4571

VA

Alabama
Henry Moody, Loan Guaranty Officer
Ralph Strickland, Property Management Chief
474 South Court Street
Montgomery, AL 36104
(205) 832-7193

Alaska
Curtis Brantley, Loan Guaranty Officer
Ed Hull, Property Management Chief
235 East 8th Street
Anchorage, AK 99501
(907) 271-2215

Arizona
William Schaeffer, Property Management Chief
3225 North Central Avenue
Phoenix, AZ 85012
(602) 241-2748

Arkansas
Wilma Graham, Loan Guaranty Officer
Ed Johnson, Property Management Chief
Post Office Box 1280, Fort Roots
North Little Rock, AR 72115
(501) 378-5420

California
Paul Schikal, Loan Guaranty Officer
Angie Wild, Property Management Chief
Federal Building
11000 Wilshire Boulevard
Los Angeles, CA 90024
(213) 209-7838

Charles Bidondo, Loan Guaranty Officer
Peter O'Sullivan, Property Management Chief
211 Main Street
San Francisco, CA 94105
(415) 974-0730

Colorado
Julius Williams, Loan Guaranty Officer
George Tucker, Property Management Chief
44 Union Boulevard
Box 25126
Denver, CO 80225
(303) 980-2601

Connecticut
Cleve Bell, Loan Guaranty Officer
Susan Labins, Property Management Chief
450 Main Street
Hartford, CT 06103
(203) 240-3387

District of Columbia
James Nalitz, Loan Guaranty Officer
Walter Covington, Property Management Chief
941 North Capital Street, NE
Washington, DC 20421
(202) 275-0611

Florida
Bill Cipolla, Loan Guaranty Officer
Post Office Box 1437
St. Petersburg, FL 33731
(813) 893-3409

Georgia
Wayne Beck, Loan Guaranty Officer
Howard Yeager, Property Management Chief
730 Peachtree Street, NE
Atlanta, GA 30365
(404) 347-3474

Hawaii
Thomas Serocca, Loan Guaranty Officer,
  Property Management Chief
Post Office Box 50188
Honolulu, HI 96850
(808) 546-2160

Idaho
Charles Brioschi, Loan Guaranty Officer
Ray Sims, Property Management Chief
550 West Fort Street
Boise, ID 83724
(208) 334-1367

Illinois
Alan Schneider, Loan Guaranty Officer
David Stelzner, Property Management Chief
536 South Clark Street
Post Office Box 8136
Chicago, IL 60680
(312) 353-4068

Indiana
Frank Kuehn, Loan Guaranty Officer
Robert Amt, Property Management Chief
575 Pennsylvania Street
Indianapolis, IN 46204
(317) 226-7827

Iowa
Jack Rivers, Loan Guaranty Officer
Raymond Morris, Property Management Chief
210 Walnut Street
Des Moines, IA 50309
(515) 284-4657

Kansas
Danny Cross, Loan Guaranty Officer
George Lyon, Property Management Chief
VA Regional Office and Medical Center
901 George Washington Boulevard
Wichita, KS 67211
(316) 269-6728

Kentucky
Michele Culp, Loan Guaranty Officer
Richard Sloan, Property Management Chief
600 Federal Place
Louisville, KY 40202
(502) 582-5866

Louisiana
Paul Griener, Loan Guaranty Officer
Darryl Crum, Property Management Chief
701 Loyola Avenue
New Orleans, LA 70113
(504) 589-6459

Maine
John Bales, Loan Guaranty Officer
Jack Donovan, Property Management Chief
VA Medical and Regional Office
Togus, ME 04330
(207) 623-5434

Maryland
Judy Eagan, Loan Guaranty Officer
Don Dennehy, Property Management Chief
31 Hopkins Plaza
Baltimore, MD 21201
(301) 962-4467

Massachusetts
Arthur Snyder, Loan Guaranty Officer
Dennis Keefe, Property Management Chief
John F. Kennedy Building
Boston, MA 02203
(617) 565-3027

Michigan
Stan Brown, Loan Guaranty Officer
Mike Johnson, Property Management Chief
477 Michigan Avenue
Detroit, MI 48226
(313) 226-7561

Minnesota
Don Munro, Loan Guaranty Officer
Dennis Johnson, Property Management Chief
VA Regional Office and Insurance Center
Fort Snelling

St. Paul, MN 55111
(612) 725-3054

Mississippi
Ron Veltman, Loan Guaranty Officer
Ron Stowers, Property Management Chief
100 West Capital Street
Jackson, MS 39269
(601) 960-4840

Missouri
James Mullins, Loan Guaranty Officer
Gerald Jones, Property Management Chief
1520 Market Street
St. Louis, MO 63103
(314) 539-3144

Montana
Albert Olsen, Loan Guaranty Officer
Ruth Smith, Property Management Chief
VA Regional Office and Medical Center
Fort Harrison, MT 59636
(406) 442-6410

Nebraska
Harold Matthes, Loan Guaranty Officer
Carol Swan, Property Management Chief
100 Centennial Mall, N.
Lincoln, NE 68508
(402) 471-5031

New Hampshire
Bruce Carstarphen, Loan Guaranty Officer
Ray Arocha, Property Management Chief
275 Chestnut Street
Manchester, NH 03101
(603) 666-7656

New Jersey
Elmer DeRitter, Loan Guaranty Officer
Russ Williams, Property Management Chief
20 Washington Place
Newark, NJ 07102
(201) 645-3607

New Mexico
Terry Niendorf, Loan Guaranty Officer
Jean McKinney, Property Management Chief
500 Gold Avenue, SW
Albuquerque, NM 87102
(505) 766-2214

New York
Keith Boerner, Loan Guaranty Officer
Mike Meyer, Property Management Chief
111 West Huron Street
Buffalo, NY 14202
(716) 846-5295

New York
Gerald Prizeman, Loan Guaranty Officer
William Rooney, Property Management Chief
252 7th Avenue at 24th Street
New York, NY 10001
(212) 620-6421

North Carolina
John Koivisto, Loan Guaranty Officer
Allen Smith, Property Management Chief
251 North Main Street
Winston-Salem, NC 27155
(919) 761-3494

Ohio
Thomas Vickroy, Loan Guaranty Officer
Jim Haugh, Property Management Chief
1240 East 9th Street
Cleveland, OH 44199
(216) 522-3583

Oklahoma
Jean Mathis, Loan Guaranty Officer
Harvey Sweet, Property Management Chief
125 Main Street
Muskogee, OK 74401
(918) 687-2161

Oregon
Phyllis Somers, Loan Guaranty Officer
Richard Lewis, Property Management Chief
1220 SW Third Avenue
Portland, OR 97204
(503) 326-2484

Pennsylvania
Richard Kesteven, Loan Guaranty Officer
Steve Loughnane, Property Management Chief
VA Regional Office and Insurance Center
5000 Wissahickon Avenue
Philadelphia, PA 19101
(215) 951-5508

Carl Rueter, Al Curotola
VA Regional Office
1000 Liberty Avenue
Pittsburgh, PA 15222
(412) 644-4508

South Carolina
Carl Rueter, Loan Guaranty Officer
Al Curotola, Property Management Chief
1801 Assembly Street
Columbia, SC 29201
(803) 765-5154

Tennessee
Kenneth Harvey, Loan Guaranty Officer
Billy Bushulen, Property Management Chief
110 9th Avenue, South
Nashville, TN 37203
(615) 251-5241

Texas

Mike McReaken, Loan Guaranty Officer
Rosemary Kissel, Property Management Chief
2515 Murworth Drive
Houston, TX 77054
(713) 660-4384

Rod Locke, Loan Guaranty Officer
Bill Carr, Property Management Chief
1400 North Valley Mills Drive
Waco, TX 76799
(817) 757-6869

Utah

Gilbert Yocky, Loan Guaranty Officer
Gerald Overstreet, Property Management Chief
Post Office Box 11500
Salt Lake City, UT 84147
(801) 524-5986

Virginia

Bill Hogan, Loan Guaranty Officer
Robert Gibson, Property Management Chief
210 Franklin Road, SW
Roanoke, VA 24011
(703) 982-6141

Washington

Lauris Whitehead, Loan Guaranty Officer
Cheryle Lang, Property Management Chief
915 Second Avenue
Seattle, WA 98174
(206) 442-7014

West Virginia

Robert Shearin, Loan Guaranty Officer
Margo Keyser, Property Management Chief
640 4th Avenue
Huntington, WV 25701
(304) 529-5046

Wisconsin
Thomas Malta, Loan Guaranty Officer
Susan Lofton, Property Management Chief
Post Office Box 6
Milwaukee, WI 53295
(414) 382-5060

Puerto Rico
Peter Wells, Loan Guaranty Officer
Linda Carr, Property Management Chief
General Post Office Box 4867
San Juan, PR 00936
(809) 498-5216

FmHA

National Office
U.S. Department of Agriculture
Farmers Home Administration
Washington, DC 20250
(202) 382-1452

Alabama
Aronov Building, Room 717
474 South Court Street
Montgomery, AL 36104
(205) 832-7077

Alaska
634 South Bailey, Suite 103
Palmer, AK 99645
(907) 745-2176

Arizona
201 E. Indianola, Suite 275
Phoenix, AZ 85012
(602) 241-5086

Arkansas
Post Office Box 2778
Little Rock, AR 72203
(501) 378-6281

California
194 West Main Street, Suite F
Woodland, CA 95695-2195
(916) 666-3382

Colorado
655 Parfet Street
Room E 100
Lakewood, CO 80215
(303) 236-2854

Connecticut
Connecticut is served by the Delaware office.
See Delaware.

Delaware
2319 South Dupont Highway
Dover, DE 19901
(302) 697-0308

District of Columbia
The District of Columbia is served by the
Delaware office. See Delaware.

Florida
Post Office Box 2310
Gainesville, FL 32602-1310
(904) 376-3218

Georgia
Stephens Federal Building
355 East Hancock Avenue
Athens, GA 30610
(404) 546-2162

Hawaii
Federal Building, Room 311
154 Waianuenue Avenue
Hilo, HI 96720
(808) 961-4781

Idaho
3232 Elder Street
Boise, ID 83705
(208) 334-1301

Illinois
Illini Plaza, Suite 103
1817 South Neil Street
Champaign, IL 61820
(217) 398-5235

Indiana
5975 Lakeside Boulevard
Indianapolis, IN 46278
(317) 290-3100

Iowa
873 Federal Building
210 Walnut Street
Des Moines, IA 50309
(515) 284-4663

Kansas
444 SE Quincy Street, Room 176
Topeka, KS 66683
(913) 295-2870

Kentucky
333 Waller Avenue
Lexington, KY 40504
(606) 233-2733

Louisiana
3727 Government Street
Alexandria, LA 71302
(318) 473-7920

Maine
USDA Office Building
Orono, ME 04473
(207) 581-3400

Maryland
Maryland is served by the Delaware office.
See Delaware.

Massachusetts
451 West Street
Amherst, MA 01002
(413) 253-3471

Michigan
1405 S. Harrison Road, Room 209
East Lansing, MI 48823
(517) 337-6631

Minnesota
410 Farm Credit Building
375 Jackson Street
St. Paul, MN 55101-1853

Mississippi
Federal Building, Suite 831
Jackson, MS 30269
(601) 965-4316

Missouri
555 Vandiver Drive
Columbia, MO 65202
(314) 875-5237

Montana
Post Office Box 850
Bozeman, MT 59771
(406) 587-6787

Nebraska
Federal Building, Room 308
100 Centennial Mall North
Lincoln, NE 68508
(402) 437-5551

New Hampshire
141 Main Street
Montpelier, VT 05602
(802) 233-2371

New Jersey
100 High Street, Suite 100
Mt. Holly, NJ 08060
(609) 267-3090

New Mexico
Federal Building, Room 3414
517 Gold Avenue, SW
Albuquerque, NM 87102
(505) 766-2462

New York
James Hanley Federal Building
Room 871
100 South Clinton Street
Syracuse, NY 13260
(315) 423-5290

North Carolina
310 New Bern Avenue
Room 525
Raleigh, NC 27601
(919) 790-2731

North Dakota
Post Office Box 1737
Bismarck, ND 58502
(701) 250-4781

Ohio
Federal Building, Room 507
200 North High Street
Columbus, OH 43215
(614) 469-5606

Oklahoma
USDA Agricultural Center Building
Stillwater, OK 74074
(405) 624-4250

Oregon
Federal Building, Room 1590
1220 SW 3rd Avenue
Portland, OR 97204
(503) 221-2731

Pennsylvania
Federal Building, Room 730
Post Office Box 905
Harrisburg, PA 17108-0905
(717) 782-4476

Puerto Rico
New San Juan Center Building
Room 501
159 Carlos Chardon Street
Hato Rey, PR 00918-5481
(809) 766-5095

Rhode Island
451 West Street
Amherst, MA 01002
(413) 253-3471

South Carolina
Strom Thurmond Federal Building
Room 1007
1835 Assembly Street
Columbia, SC 29201
(803) 765-5163

South Dakota
Federal Building, Room 308
200 4th Street, SW
Huron, SD 57350
(605) 353-1430

Tennessee
Federal Building
U.S. Courthouse, Room 538
801 Broadway
Nashville, TN 37203
(615) 736-7341

Texas
Federal Building, Suite 102
101 South Main
Temple, TX 76501
(817) 774-1301

Utah
Wallace F. Bennett Federal Building
Room 5438
125 South State Street
Salt Lake City, UT 84138
(801) 524-4063

Vermont
141 Main Street
Montpelier, VT 05602
(802) 233-2371

Virgin Islands
The Virgin Islands is served by
Vermont. See Vermont.

Virginia
Federal Building, Room 8213
400 North 8th Street
Richmond, VA 23240
(804) 771-2451

Washington
Post Office Box 2427
Wenatchee, WA 98807
(509) 662-4352

West Virginia
Post Office Box 678
Morgantown, WV 26505
(304) 291-4791

Wisconsin
1257 Main Street
Stevens Point, WI 54481
(715) 341-5900

Wyoming
Post Office Box 820
Casper, WY 82602
(307) 261-5271

INDEX